BREAKTHROUGH

How To Design Your Life

Remove anxiety, end suffering, get clarity and connection, plan a happy life

by

JOE THOMSETT

Copyright © 2023 JOE THOMSETT.

All rights reserved. This book or any portion thereof may not be reproduced or used in any manner whatsoever without the express written permission of the publisher except for the use of brief quotations in a book review.

ISBN: 978-1-7395331-0-6 (Paperback)

Publishing company: Coevolve Publishing

*God, grant me the serenity
to accept the things I cannot change,
the courage to change the things I can,
and the wisdom to know the difference.*

- The Serenity Prayer

CONTENTS

PART 1 - INTRODUCTION 1

    INTRODUCTION 2

PART 2 - TYRANNY 16

    REDISCOVERING OURSELVES 17

    REMOVING NEGATIVE CHILDHOOD SCRIPTS............29

    UNDERSTANDING SOCIAL PROGRAMMING..............45

PART 3 - THE DESERT 53

    ESCAPING THE PROGRAMMED WORLD.....................54

    LOSING MY DAD 63

    FINDING MYSELF 74

    JOURNALING FOR MY LIFE 81

    FINDING LOVE 90

    NOW I'M A DAD 98

A PIECE OF YOUR SOUL IN ALL THINGS....................108

FAITH IN A HIGHER POWER..115

WHAT'S ESSENTIAL IS INVISIBLE TO THE EYE..........125

PART 4 - LESSONS LEARNED 134

TO DO PUSH-UPS, DO PUSH-UPS................................135

DEPTH IS GREATER THAN BREADTH 140

DOING IS LEARNING..147

REMOVE 90% OF EVERYTHING 154

YOUR ENGAGEMENT PATTERNS DETERMINE YOUR DAY 159

LIFESTYLE DESIGN IS ESSENTIAL 168

TIME IS ALL YOU HAVE 174

DECIDE, TAKE STEPS, ADJUST 182

CONCLUSION..189

PART 1

INTRODUCTION

INTRODUCTION

Won't sacrifice my soul

Won't sacrifice my soul for your powerpoint bullshit. Won't sacrifice my soul for status updates, or progress reports. Won't sacrifice my soul for dreary days where everything is a copy of a copy of a copy - "Pass the salt. Did you get the memo? What shall we watch tonight?" Won't sacrifice my soul for a career path and stale biscuits, or for Clive telling me that I have potential but need to put my head down and grind for a few years longer, in order to demonstrate my commitment to the company. Won't sacrifice my soul because this is how it is and it's what everybody does. Won't sacrifice my soul for status, or prestige, or good wine and a compliment from Robert the multi-millionaire vaping store mogul. Won't sacrifice my soul to be known as a someone to my friends, or sports colleagues, or business owners at the closed networking group. Won't sacrifice my soul for possessions. Won't sacrifice my soul for cars. Or houses. Or hidden knowledge.

But we all do at some stage.

Some of us understand instantly, while others get it after a few jobs and a lot of bad coffee. Most people who escape get lured back in by a childhood siren song echoing mum, or dad, or an impressive professor determining what's proper and what matters and what we should strive for. Others still, they only get it at the grave.

Don't be the last example.

Understand who you uniquely are

A sceptic reading this might scoff at the immaturity of thinking and suggest I grow up and realise the responsibilities that come with life, or conflate my desire to not compromise my being with not wanting

INTRODUCTION

to work. To the first point, I say you have a responsibility to live life in accordance with your idiosyncratic nature, and that you should spend time understanding what that is. And in respect of the second point, not at all. I've got admiration for the 9-5er who does their work because it's exactly what they want to do. Or because the trade-off means they can spend time on those things that make their heart sing; like playing with their kids, running, cooking, or travel. And I have admiration for the creative solopreneur putting a little bit of themselves into each piece of work they produce. Or the business woman impacting thousands of lives.

The point is not to avoid work, or work all the time, or work for a company, or work for yourself, or some other prescriptive cookie cutter cliché. The point is to understand who you uniquely are, what it is you want to do, and how it is you want to live, so you can design a life that strives for it.

The icky veneer covering us

As children, we didn't think about any of it. We just did what we were compelled to do. Want to play football in the garden? Or spend time talking with your best mates about the silly things and the deep stuff within the same conversation? Or try to solve little puzzles for fun? You did.

Growing up comes with prescriptions and conformities that slowly ebb away at our natural predispositions. Whether it's the regularity and hierarchy of the industrial school system, or the peer pressure that being with hundreds of your age group brings. Or it's transfer to the corporate world, approximating the training ground you just left behind.

Each hammer blow chips away at, softens and reforms us, until we've been remade, unrecognisable from our being and dissatisfied with the transmutation, unable to articulate exactly what it is, but able to sense an icky veneer covering us and censoring us from connection to our true selves.

INTRODUCTION

And the hilarity of it all is, as we look around, we find the feeling prevalent and permeating the population. We are not the only ones. The matrix is everywhere. We are the middle of the bell curve, placed firmly in the centre by the piercing arrows of our childhood scripts, our mechanised training, and deluded societal conformities and expectations.

Middle of the bell curve is mimicry

Middle of the bell curve is mimicry. It's millions of people with the same corporate double-speak, wearing the same dull suits, polishing the same powerpoint slides or excel spreadsheets, eating the same mass-produced lunch baguettes, chasing the same status and monetary accolades, getting slowly sick in the same predictable fashion, approaching death with the same desires and regrets, way past having the ability to do anything about it.

A copy of a copy of a copy.

PART 1 - INTRODUCTION

Tyranny of the self

This is tyranny of the self, coercion of the soul, a twisting of the very fabric of your being. It's the knot in your stomach that you try to ignore, or worse, accept. It's presenting a hollowed-out version of yourself so frequently, that you've forgotten who you are.

Except in the moments where the web of entanglement no longer has you. Those brief interludes. Maybe you're thrust into the single-minded nature of a competitive sport. Maybe you're in a temporary state of solitude, devoid of digital distraction and pervasive peers, alone with your thoughts, your metaphorical makeup slowly washing away; and so you get a brief glimpse of yourself, your true self.

Of course, you'll likely not realise this the first many times; you'll just feel good, or easy, or in flow. But accumulate enough moments, and something begins to stir in you. From experience, it's not a, 'this is who I am' feeling. Rather, it's a, 'this is who I'm not' realisation. And it's not a feeling that manifests all warm

INTRODUCTION

and fuzzy and serene and enlightening. It's deep-seated angst. It's dread. It's being in your normal setting with your skin crawling and heart pounding and the constant urge to get up and sprint or scream or blast out of your body, like your life depends on it. It's nauseating. It's itchy. It's pit of your stomach sick.

And for a long time it's confusing. If you're in good job or good relationship with good prospects, in line with the societal rhetoric du jour; yet your internal dialogue is screaming at you at the top of it's lungs, frenzied by the dreariness and monotony and misalignment of it all, you can feel like you're going a bit mad.

You are not mad

Rest assured, you are not mad. And you are not the only one feeling this way. There are millions of us, daily adopting the mask of conformity, unknowing or unwilling to break through and break free, unable to reclaim our being as our own and to live in alignment with it.

PART 1 - INTRODUCTION

Without a predisposition to be comfortable in disorder, to stumble and fumble and tinker to change; or without a framework to follow, the story ends here. The suffering of tyranny is easier to bear than suffering the unknown. And so many souls accept the beautiful moments as the exception and the angst as the norm.

Others can't ignore the angst and so vow to make a change. A holiday, travel sabbatical, start-up, consulting gig, career change, family, material purchase or new hobby. The change can often be enough for people to develop temporary amnesia or a system reset from the misalignment problem, and continue this punctuation cycle in perpetuity to the grave.

Yet some people manage to catalyse a change into an escape from self-imposed tyranny. This leap is liberating at first, as you go from corporate slave to free-spirited flaneur. However, soon enough, the familiar feeling of anxiety and uneasiness comes creeping up again. Why? Because it's one thing to

INTRODUCTION

know what you shouldn't be doing; it's another thing completely to know what you should be doing. So it's out of tyranny, into the desert.

The desert

The desert is dry, expansive, without signposts or pathways. It's full of traps and poisons and lacks sustenance. It's weary to traverse, and the constant strain conjures illusions that you chase.

It's taking on consulting gigs for money only, convinced that some point soon you'll do more of what makes your heart sing. It's doing twenty different projects to increase your options, struggling to understand where to focus. It's travelling to Thailand to be a digital nomad, unsure why, except it's something different to try. It's climbing the corporate ladder, chasing promotions, building for a cushy retirement and hoping you'll be well enough to enjoy it. It's watching endless Youtube videos and reading countless Twitter threads, looking for the information nugget that helps you find

PART 1 - INTRODUCTION

your purpose. It's productivity hacking, setting up Notion templates and optimising your day, without knowing what you're doing it for. It's running out of runway and starting over again. It's anxiety, and upset, and frustration, and hopelessness, and a constant questioning of whether or not you've done the right thing leaving the status quo behind, or not leaving it at all. It's missing out on leisure, interests, connection, relationships, aliveness, and love. These are the mirages of the desert.

It's all of these things, and none of them, depending on who you are.

It's the sobering realisation that you're in the desert. It's the lingering untrue stickiness that unless you're some quantifiable measure of success, you've made a loser decision and have failed. It's wondering whether to return to the tyrannical self, accepting the uneasiness and self-loathing that accompanies it. And it's developing the courage to try things, stacking lessons, accumulating wisdom, until one day you break through,

INTRODUCTION

and understand what it's all about. Out of the desert, into paradise.

Breakthrough

Breakthrough is living such that the moments where the web of entanglement no longer has you is expanded. It's freedom from the attachment of outside expectations and conformities. It's living in resonance with your being, and building on your natural talents to pursue your idealised-self. It's taking a holistic view of your life, interests, relationships and community and designing it in accord with who you are. It's understanding that the mainstream zeitgeist is manufactured and mimetic and that listening to your heart, thinking for yourself and adhering to a set of morally good principles is the timeless way to live with serenity.

It's understanding that time runs out, that every day you have less of it, and you have no idea when it ends. It's building maximum agency over your time, and figuring

PART 1 - INTRODUCTION

out the things you want to spend it on, in order to have a life well-lived.

It's realising that you'll find yourself in the desert from time to time, embracing it, welcoming it, and using it as a lesson to escape the descent into tyranny and continue to ascend into the realms of paradise.

It's not a new set of questions. It's been with us since we emerged. What's life about? How should I live it? What's my purpose? Why am I here?

It's in the lessons of Christianity and other religions. It's in the works of philosophers. In the internet age, it's been discussed by Tim Ferris, Cal Newport, Naval Ravikant, and many others. It's in movements like Minimalism, FIRE (financial independence, retire early), indie hacking and the creator economy. It's in movies, like The Matrix, Amelie, and Intouchables. It's in books, such as The Bible, The Little Prince, The Prophet and Deep work.

INTRODUCTION

It's in the places you look for it at the time you feel the urge to search for it.

And when you get the urge, I pray that you search for it.

A personal essay

This is not a technical or research driven book. I'm not attempting to give you a practical framework to follow, a five step series that promises you enlightenment.

Instead, it's a personal essay, where I explore my experiences with stumbling from tyranny to the desert, attempting to break through. It's intimate and conversational. I hope it's relatable. It's a call to arms. It's me shouting from my lungs for you to grab your life and make it your own, to avoid the siren songs of parental, professor and peer pressures, and to breakthrough, before it's too late. It's a reminder that time is a non-renewable resource, that you know in your bones what to avoid and where to explore, and that you should plan your life holistically, aiming for your

PART 1 - INTRODUCTION

north star, underpinned by morality. It's a reminder that to escape the tyranny of living out of sync with your being, following societal prescriptions and delusions, you need the courage to go into the desert, to embrace the uncertainty of the unknown, and to tinker until you find what's right. It's my shared learnings that your health, environment, relationships, interests, and love all make up large parts of the tapestry of your life. And they're often left, deemed insignificant in comparison to career and status and prestige, which is the root of a lot of unhappiness.

Into the desert we go.

PART 2
TYRANNY

REDISCOVERING OURSELVES

Introduction

We want to live our lives engaged, dancing with vitality, fully expressing ourselves. But in the humdrum of daily life, stuck on the treadmill, doing all the things we've been told to do, we become untethered from that which gives us joy and disconnected from our being. We lose meaning in the little things and meaning in the big picture. As a result, we end up disengaged, alive but not living, mindlessly following the paths put before us, anxious about how we feel inside, or worse, totally numb to it. It doesn't have to be this way. As children, we did things that engaged us, enlivened us, and enraptured us. We hadn't yet lost our innocence, or been told what we should or shouldn't do with our lives, or how we should spend our time. If we look back, we can re-discover those moments, re-connect ourselves to them, and extrapolate and apply the lessons into our adult lives. We do this by figuring out the patterns - what did we love, what were we good at, what uplifted us? – and re-do them as adults. We either re-do the activity – for example, a sport. Or we apply the higher order principle the activity implies – for example, daily intense movement. The re-discovery and re-application of these things in our lives engages us and makes them meaningful. And the re-tethering to ourselves the activities induce seeps into the rest of our lives, making us more aware, alive and in play.

Weekend holiday brighton hotel romp

I have a brother and sister, 11 and 9 years older than me respectively. Big gap. I joke that I'm the product of a weekend holiday Brighton hotel romp. The best kind of baby – conceived in a moment of magic, with all the right ingredients, but in a crazy shaken-up mish-mash manner.

PART 2 - TYRANNY

We had very different upbringings. When I was born, my parents were going through financial turmoil; with my Dad's family business bankrupted, and the builder of our house closing down after conveniently taking a large advance payment from the family. Bastards.

I used to go to my nan and grandads house after school. They were the best grandparents. The kind who fed you too much and fattened you up, who played games with you and encouraged you. I'd arrive to a handful of cheesy biscuits and play with their dog, Penny. We'd eat dinner; old school meals like toad in the hole, chips and corned beef, or roast chicken, potatoes and vegetables. My nan made her own gravy, and I'd have a cup of it with meals, which is insane, and resulted in weight gain, and not recommended! We'd then play cards – Whist or Rummy – before mum collected me and took me home.

Cigarettes and alcohol

Dad would be at the pub, drinking away his sorrows and puffing on cigarettes, before coming home and continuing his descent, replacing beer with wine, laying on the couch, lost in the density of his smoky sorrow. He had a profound impact on me, positively and negatively. He was the smartest man I knew, and the most wasteful. He was loving and hurtful. He was difficult. I was desperate to be around him, to be acknowledged by him, but scared I'd step out of line and be verbally cascaded. I loved him, wanted nothing more than to be with him, but was terrified by him. He simultaneously set scripts that contributed to my tyranny, and gave me the tools to escape to the desert.

Rodmersham squash club

At 13, my friend Mark introduced me to squash. My dad, brother and sister used to play, so I was keen to try. It was magic. I went on Saturdays. My friend Guy came too. We trained, joined the leagues, made the team, and generally fell in love with the sport.

PART 2 - TYRANNY

Saturdays became nearly every day. We added in fitness training, coached each other in games, and dreamt about getting better. Squash was fundamental to my development, and encouraging me to go was one of the best decisions my parents made.

Squash is like physical chess. You need strategy, endurance, adaptability, resilience, and heart. Going deep into the sport laid some of the foundations for the rest of my life. It gave me the ability to focus, to play solo, to go deep, to work with team mates, to coach and encourage, and to trust myself.

And more fundamentally, I loved it. As children and adolescents, we're drawn to things, do them, and if we love them, stick with them. There's no complex equation to figure out. No opportunity-cost scorecard, no consideration of societal expectations or careers. We just do it. Picasso famously said, "Every child is an artist. The problem is how to remain an artist once we grow up." Doing what you love is art. It's an expression of who you are. And there's no higher art than body, mind and spiritual alignment. Breakthrough is living Picasso's understanding. It's finding the artist within you and embodying that as an adult interacting in the world.

Re-discovery

I stopped squash fully around age 24, after suffering a bad leg injury. I stupidly tried to do an 8 mile run and a tough squash match one after the other, and suffered the consequences. So I put it on the shelf and forgot about it. At 35, once a week I dropped my daughter off at my mum's house, which was near where I used to play. My best friend asked me to come down and get on court. So I did. And I loved it. In an instant the magic returned. All the same feelings. The joy, camaraderie, focus, strategy and persistence.

My leg held up, and I haven't looked back since. After re-discovering squash, I re-integrated it into my life. First of all slowly, and then after review and considering where to spend time in my life, as a key activity.

Introduction to tools

I would never have re-integrated squash into my life without lifestyle planning – how to view life holistically, what to focus on, and how to allocate time. The idea has been discussed by many people, probably none more so than author Cal Newport.

Lifestyle planning is fundamental. It's part of a toolkit that helps you live a life in line with your Being – understanding what engages you, figuring out how to do more of it, and saying no to other things. You look at the categories that matter most to you, such as environment, work, health, relationships and hobbies, and the key activities you want to pursue in each category, and then figure out how to get there.

Squash as an activity is great, and I get deep joy when doing it. But when I look more generally, I see the meta pattern that I love movement. Whether it's walking, running, working out or sport. Or when I'm mentally moving; such as learning, conversing, piecing together an idea, or thinking on my feet. Without movement, I'm back in tyranny. This is an example of what I call an engagement pattern. Movement engages me with life, it uplifts me, I'm a better person with it. By consciously thinking how to integrate movement into my life, and applying it, I'm more connected, I'm happier. Figuring out these engagement patterns and combining them with lifestyle planning is a superpower that helps you live a life of vitality.

How to rediscover them

You can do the same thing. What are things you loved doing as a child, before things got foggy with what your parents said you should do, or what school told you to think about, or what society said was important? And what things were you doing later in life, where you felt more in flow, alive, or when you had a sense of freedom?

There are a few ways to explore this. You can:

- **Reflect on childhood activities and interests.** I loved squash and running. I enjoyed outdoor

PART 2 - TYRANNY

adventures. I wrote silly poems. I enjoyed talking with my best friend. I enjoyed maths, french and religious studies at school. I loved a couple of teenage holidays by the beach.

- **Consider your childhood dreams and aspirations.** At one point I wanted to be a professional squash player. And then a writer. Or a mathematician. And then an entrepreneur.

- **Remember who your childhood heroes or role models were.** The footballer Ronaldinho. The squash player Amr Shabana. The writer Paulo Coelho. 'Will' in the movie Good Will Hunting. 'Neo' in the movie 'The Matrix.'

- **Talk with childhood friends and family.** I spoke with my mum, brother and best friend. My mum always mentions my writing. My brother talks about autonomy and a sense of freedom. My best friend talks about my preference to find meaning in the things I do.

- **Consider the same questions as a young adult or any time you had more freedom.** As a young adult leaving home, I listened to and felt moved by music that explored our humanness, and movies that did the same. And I read a ton of personal development, pop psychology and decision-making books with my brother, taking copious notes.

You may have other ways too. Going over old journals, watching old videos, revisiting physical locations and reconnecting with a particular feeling or sensation. The point is to carve out time to undertake the exercise, and to reconnect with the things that sparked curiosity for you and brought you joy.

Does any particular activity or interest keep coming up? Are you doing it somehow in your life? For me, it was squash and running, and I've made sure it stays.

Are there any deeper engagement patterns at play? They are the fundamental building blocks of personal

PART 2 - TYRANNY

contentment and fulfilment. I identified I like to be in motion – physical, mental, spiritual – I feel stuck without it, and so I design my life to embody it as much as possible.

If it matters to you, it matters

If it's important to you, it matters. As humans, we're meaning making machines, we invent stories. The sad reality is that the majority of us follow stories already written for us, suffering in silence, frustrated and unaware, rather than authoring our own lives. Authoring our own stories gives us purpose, depth and fulfilment. It makes us engage with life, play with it and dance with it.

It's not silly to do activities or extract principles from the things you loved to do or was interested in as a kid. The opposite, actually. Unless you had a highly traumatic childhood, there would have been pockets of time where you did things just because you wanted to, because you were drawn to them. That's the pull of

REDISCOVERING OURSELVES

your individual being, the part of you that's you. Don't ignore it, protect it. They are representations of more fundamental activities that quench your spirit and fill you up. Figuring out how to integrate them into your life will give you personal meaning and purpose and will take you out of the tyranny of living life on someone else's terms, quietly frustrated and bent out of shape, into flow, fulfilment, serenity and being.

Time to get started. Review your childhood.

REMOVING NEGATIVE CHILDHOOD SCRIPTS

Holding us back

We want to live our best, authentic lives, where we're making good choices that help us far into the future. But sometimes our negative childhood programming holds us back. We overcome that by revisiting the decisions we made as survival strategies when demands were made of us, realising them for what they are, seeing how they manifest for us as adults, and proactively moving past them.

Making unconscious decisions or reacting involuntarily in service of our child ego can really hold us back. Understanding what causes this and moving past it opens up the possibility to thrive.

REMOVING NEGATIVE CHILDHOOD SCRIPTS

Decent childhood

I had a decent enough childhood. I got to play in the garden or ride my bike, play football and take up squash, and my parents loved me. I was driving at 18, and had been working different part-time jobs as a teenager to have a few coins in my pocket to do things. I had my first girlfriend at sweet sixteen, and I made friends with people who are my closest friends today.

I remember this one time, my best friend Guy and I, up in a little box room in my parents house, loading a rap song called 'Slow Jamz' on the computer, each taking turns to try and recite the rap, laughing at each other as the words got faster and faster. Back then, we used to have to take the tracks from a website online and burn them onto a CD. Computers were so slow and clunky that turning one on sounded like a rocket ship about to take off, and you'd just sit there with quiet anticipation until you could start using it.

I have some wonderful childhood memories. And in childhood and adolescence lie the keys to our energy patterns, what we're naturally drawn to, and the things we truly love before we're told what to love by everybody else. But what also exists there are handcuffs that keep us in mental tyranny, stopping us as adults from making healthy decisions and doing things that might lead us to an abundant life – our childhood scripts.

Childhood scripts and survival strategies

Our scripts are the decisions we subconsciously make as kids to deal with situations where we're attempting to gain love or avoid the loss of it. They're little survival strategies turned into mental programs. And if the program runs often enough or deep enough as kids, it stays in mind. As an adult, if you're in a situation that makes you feel how you felt as a kid with your survival strategies, then the program will run again. Scripts can be created from copying behaviour, being labelled something, being suggested too, and being demanded of.

REMOVING NEGATIVE CHILDHOOD SCRIPTS

If you had a perfect childhood with healthy parents without any scripts of their own running, you may not have many yourself. If you had a tragic childhood, with abuse or something worse, always in a state of survival, you'll have many.

Most kids will have reasonably good childhoods and still develop a number of scripts that might hold them back. If one of your parents had an 'I'm right and everyone else is an idiot' operating style, or an 'I'm a victim and everyone is out to get me' operating style, then you'll likely have created little survival programs to deal with the times when that personality manifested itself in your parent. You gave up your true needs in order to get love or avoid the loss of love.

As adults, these scripts can invisibly shape our self image, and bleed into the decisions we make, putting us on different paths to the ones we really want to take. For example, you might wake up twenty years later and think, 'why did I decide to work in investment banking? I hate investment banking!' There's a good chance you were serving your child ego, looking for the love of a parent – acceptance – whether you knew it or not.

Table tennis memories

Growing up, I loved my Dad dearly. I wanted to spend time with him. He had a presence about him that I was drawn to. Like he knew things that others didn't, that there was something more to him than everyone else. It was rare we'd do things together, but when we did, I'd long for it to continue. Once, he made a table tennis table out of plywood, and we played a few times in the garden. That's one of my best memories, because for a few moments, whatever troubled him had left, and he was just having fun with his kid, child-like himself. Or a few times we made a little fire and cooked marshmallows together. Those were innocent, pure moments.

But my Dad was troubled too. His Dad was a reargunner in world war 2, got shot down, survived, was captured, and escaped. After the war, for years he suffered with post-traumatic stress, and he used to take it out on his boys, beating them. My Dad, the youngest of the boys, was the only one not beaten, but he still saw it. My Dad always drank and smoked, and was pretty successful by conventional measures, running a big family logistics business and renovating and selling houses. Until one day the business lost its biggest contract, bankrupting it, and at the same time a dodgy house builder took a large upfront payment from my Dad and promptly folded, nearly bankrupting him. It's around this time I was born. In my Dad's eyes, he'd lost everything, and he plunged into a depression, filled with cigarettes and alcohol. My mum had to pick up the slack financially, and basically looked after all of us.

Be careful boy

Dad was a conundrum. He'd bring out the most worldly-wise advice, whilst laying half-drunk on the sofa. He was the smartest person I knew, yet would be working odd jobs or not at all. His being was 'do as I say, not as I do'. He was dictatorial, hierarchical, and

PART 2 - TYRANNY

ran his parent-child relationship on fear, whether he knew it or not.

I'd tip toe around him, craving his attention. But if I said something he didn't like, or looked at the clock the wrong way, he'd say 'be careful boy', or, 'one more time and me and you are gonna fall out'. And he meant it.

In Transactional Analysis, a branch of psychotherapy, this is an 'injunction', a demand. I'd modify my behaviour around him, because I didn't want to lose his love, and I didn't want confrontation. He used to smoke in the house too, all the time. I'd sit in the room with him, and cover my nose with my t-shirt. If I coughed or he got fed up with me doing it, he'd say, 'don't be such a drama queen.' So I'd do my best to stop, poisoning my lungs in order to be around him.

He always called people idiots, including us, often in a half joking manner, but always meant by him. And in anger, he'd project his disgust onto us. In Transactional

REMOVING NEGATIVE CHILDHOOD SCRIPTS

Analysis, this is known as a 'Life Position' of being 'I'm ok, you're not okay', which is when people project their problems onto others and blame them, put them down, and criticise them, to maintain their own sense of 'okay-ness'. It's the 'I'm right and you're wrong' position, and if someone questions it, in the eyes of the person subconsciously operating this way, they become the 'not okay' part, the person doing the wronging, the person doing the misunderstanding.

With this in mind, childhood and adolescence was me craving the love of my dad, tiptoeing around his scorn to avoid confrontation and conforming to conditional cues in order to win affection. I loved squash, and he was kind enough to let me play whenever I wanted to. But throughout my childhood, he never stepped on court with me, and watched me just once, leaving halfway through. I still remember it now. Him leaving was far worse than me losing the match. When I did well in maths at school, he told me my brother was a maths genius. Anything requested other than squash

PART 2 - TYRANNY

was met with the view that I was ungrateful or up to something and it was outrageous to ask. Between the ages of 16 and 18, he'd get drunk a lot. One night, going to the bed, he grabbed my arm and asked if I was on drugs (hilarious), with the usual 'be careful boy' quip when I responded with confusion and disbelief. When I got my A-level results, not getting the top marks he expected of me, he didn't talk to me for three weeks. He told me I'd waste university, so I never applied. He told me to be an accountant, so I did. When I told him I wanted to quit, he told me I could be anything I wanted, but I'd have to start paying a decent rent. I ultimately left home soon after, taking my attention with me, but sticking with a profession that ate me up, still looking for love and recognition.

My childhood scripts

This relationship created scripts for me, some of which I learned in early adulthood, some only recently. Firstly, I made decisions within the frame of pleasing my Dad. I didn't know it, but I was subconsciously chasing recognition, and concerned about his judgement. Even when I left home, I stayed in a profession I hated. And it's no coincidence that I left it, only after he'd left the country. I recently learned this comes up for me as an older adult too. If I do something for a loved one and don't feel seen, I can automatically feel slighted. That's the same program running. Secondly, as a young adult in particular, I had a tendency to not get involved with things, to stay on the periphery. That's partly a function of personality (I prefer to create deeper connections within small groups, than to be in large groups), partly a function of chasing acceptance as a kid and feeling like I wasn't getting it. It's the child ego protecting itself. Thirdly, I'd struggle to have fun and relax, to do things just because. That's judgement again.

I love you, dad

I don't write any of this to sully my Dad. Not at all. I loved him dearly. He shaped some of my strengths, and he had wonderful parts to his character. He was ridiculously funny, charming, and sharp-as-an-axe

PART 2 - TYRANNY

funny. Whenever we get too critical of our parents, it's a nice reminder to think about the age they were when they had us, and to ask ourselves how well-rounded we were at that age. We all have flaws. And our children will likely inherit some of ours; through modelling, attribution, suggestion, or demand. Even the very best parents might say or do something that impacts how their child subconsciously sees the world. And even if your parents were divine, there's plenty of people you'd have interacted with as a child who could have negatively impacted you – teachers, coaches, peers, and other parents.

Your scripts stop you living fully

Instead, I write this because if you're an adult, and you don't feel like you're living life in alignment with your being; if you feel angst or tension, or are exasperated or bored with the monotony of it all, and you don't know what to do or how to make a change, one of the reasons is you could have childhood programming holding you back. Take my personal examples. It's hard

REMOVING NEGATIVE CHILDHOOD SCRIPTS

to live life in alignment with my being, if my subconscious decision making is coloured with getting acceptance from someone else, if I'm conditioned to avoid any confrontation, and if I don't like to get too involved with things for fear of being wrong, or because of some 'me-against-the-world' non-conformity script. I left accountancy and moved into the desert, finding my way with business consultancy, travel, and contributing to a start-up. And the desert is better than the tyranny of your spirit being paralysed. But I had plenty of wrong moves, plenty of stasis and angst, and never felt in alignment with my being until I'd figured out what invisible scripts might be holding me back. There are other things to do too, like understanding the societal scripts holding you back, identifying your energy patterns, and actively designing a life that matters to you. But understanding and replacing any childhood programming is a great first step. To get to good, first remove what's bad.

Identify your childhood scripts

And how do you identify and remove limiting childhood scripts? I'm no psychotherapist, and so if you've had a traumatic time, please seek professional help. It's the most brave and kind thing you can do for yourself. For anyone who can relate to my examples, I think there are things you can proactively do to understand what limiting beliefs you have, that have arisen from childhood. I've been writing 'scripts' or 'programming' throughout this chapter, but 'belief' is another way to think about it.

Something happened repeatedly or deeply, and your neurons wired a pattern about how you see the world – a script, a program, a belief – and it's no longer serving you as an adult. The first step is to identify the belief. The second step is to recognise it for what it is; false. The third step is to update your view of the world. And the final step is to catch when that limiting belief comes up again, note how it doesn't serve you, and update your view on the situation.

REMOVING NEGATIVE CHILDHOOD SCRIPTS

The best way I know to identify your beliefs is to audit your childhood. Look for when you modified your behaviour, ultimately to gain acceptance or avoid hurt. Maybe like me, you wanted parental attention, and walked on egg shells to get it. Another way is to think about what movies and books you love, and if you identify with any of the characters. For example, I loved 'Good Will Hunting', and identified with Will – a misunderstood outsider with abilities he kept hidden, and a guard up to avoid pain and gain acceptance. I also loved 'Amelie', and identified with her – an outsider again, enjoying solitude, and seeing joy in small things. From both of those films, I can ask the question, 'why do I feel like an outsider?' Finally, if you have a partner, you can ask them if you have behaviours that always come up in negative situations; how you react or how you might treat them. Or you can journal about the negative situation and try to identify why you reacted the way you did. Once, my wife and I had a small argument about something petty. She couldn't understand my reaction. I felt really slighted. I took

PART 2 - TYRANNY

myself away for twenty minutes to journal about how I felt, and I realised her reaction stopped me feeling accepted. The same childhood script again, and I'd responded from a child ego state. I realised what had happened, explained it to her, and swiftly apologised.

Move past your limiting beliefs

Identification and acknowledgement of your limiting childhood beliefs are a great first step to living a life more aligned to your being. Moving past limiting beliefs requires doing your best to catch them when they arise, labelling them as false limiting beliefs, updating your world view, and trying to act in line with it.

This can be on the smaller stuff. For example, I'm getting better and better at catching myself when my child ego pattern fires at the feeling of a lack of acceptance or recognition from a loved one. I take a breath, put myself in their shoes, ask myself if my silly child world view is accurate, and try to update my version with a better story. Not always, but it's trending in the right direction.

And it can be on the big stuff too, like how you see yourself in the world. My life choices were subconsciously constrained by the internal pull to gain attention and love from my Dad, and by the survival decision making strategies child-me made in service of that. With that world view no longer owning me, I can paint a new picture of a life to live that feels right. It's not chasing accolades or status. Instead, it's looking at my energy patterns, what uplifts me. It's identifying the life categories that matter most, and doing that with my wife. And it's really protecting my time, spending it on those life categories and in those energy patterns.

It's away from tyranny, away from the angst and suffering of feeling constrained and constricted in the world, unable to take decisions, and unsure why you feel that way. It's in the desert, with some idea of where you're going, in more joy, enjoying the journey, with occasional glimpses of paradise.

UNDERSTANDING SOCIAL PROGRAMMING

Mimetic desire

To live a more fulfilling life, you first need to understand the social programming and dogmas you're subconsciously pulled by. Without understanding, you have inertia, where you continue doing the same thing, whittling life away, singing to a tune you didn't ask for. This programming is born from 'mimetic desire'. We desire or conform to what others have. We're subjected to social conditioning and consensus – we do what others do, because they do what others do, because we're all told it's the desirable thing to do.

Super programs

The biggest programs ('super programs') have the most general consensus. They impact all of us. Their messaging has been blasted on repeat, loudly, within our culture, so as to have become gospel. Super programs include notions like you must go to university to have a good career; a good career is something prestigious like investment banking, or law; you must buy a house and take on huge sums of debt; and our politicians and 'experts' are bastions of truth and we should accept without question what they say.

In recent years, it's become popular to compare this super programming to the film 'The Matrix,' where the majority of humans are enslaved by a few institutions of power, telling us what to think, how to feel, and how to act.

Micro programs

The smaller programs ('micro programs') have the most local consensus. They are particularly altering to each individual with their own set of circumstances. Micro programs are the social conditioning arising from our parents, peers and influencers. Social media has changed the landscape so that micro programs can arise within digital networks, rather than just local physical space. You might subconsciously desire the life and attributes of a YouTube fitness star, a Twitter technology entrepreneur, or a LinkedIn productivity guru. Your worldview and goals might be a version of their worldviews and goals, whether you know it or not.

A fulfilling life

To design a fulfilling life, you must create space from the daily grind, step back, and observe the models of desire that you're captivated by – the super programs and the micro programs. Figure out if the models you're pulled by are the things you really want. Then spend some time thinking about how you want to live. Go into your childhood and look for when you did things that gave you joy or a sense of accomplishment. Ask your partner, family and friends when you come most alive, when you fill the space with energy and vibrancy. Identify your positive energy patterns. Translate that into conscious life design, protecting

UNDERSTANDING SOCIAL PROGRAMMING

where you spend your time, and then filter out those things that don't serve it.

Programming got me

Of course, social programming got hold of me too. The super programs were there, but the micro programs held me the most. Going to school, I had no idea of alternative education or home schooling – it wasn't as prevalent as it is today. In Western society, where both parents often work, mostly without choice, school doubles up as childcare. You're sent there in the morning, get fed cheap educational sound bites, in service of getting to the next year, or to university, as opposed to educational nourishment and real world preparedness, and then packed off home to continue the pattern with standardised 'homework'. The industrial school system is a super program, but I had no idea I was in it.

I didn't go to university, because of a micro program childhood script. My dad told me I'd waste it, and the

PART 2 - TYRANNY

pull of parental acceptance outweighed the societal super program conditioning. But I did study chartered accountancy, the result of a micro and super program double-act. My Dad told me to do it. He thought it was a prestigious career, where I could make partner and earn lots of money, and maybe move into investment banking, or private equity, or some other finance derivative. I took on the parental conditioning. My Dad in turn was parroting a super program – that a good career is something like finance, that prestige and status are alluring and desirable attributes, and that earning lots of money is the same as being a success.

My foray in the desert certainly had micro program influences. I was captivated by the book 'The 4 Hour Work Week'. It opened me up to a world of lean digital entrepreneurship that I had no real idea existed. And the author Nassim Taleb got me thinking about how to create options that don't expose you to too much risk, but which might have a high pay-off. 'Indie Hackers', people running small technology or content businesses, often on their own, appealed to me for the autonomy they'd created for themselves and the apparent freedom that came with it.

You don't know what you don't know

None of these are necessarily bad things. More pertinently, I didn't know they were mimetic desires or conformities. In the desert, wearing these different hats is in some sense trying to understand who you are and what you like. If it 'feels' better than before, if there's less tension, mental tyranny and anxiety, you might be getting closer to the truth.

In my instance, I spent years subconsciously looking for parental acceptance, a cornerstone childhood script. In the desert, the Nassim Taleb influence got me too concerned with options and payoffs, when in truth I prefer deep work and substance. It's hard to build something meaningful, when you're thinking about how many options you have or that you need a payoff in days or weeks. I got caught in a loop of 'trying things'

PART 2 - TYRANNY

and binning them, often without real contact with reality. And I think it's a trap a lot of people get into. Indie Hackers got me thinking about business ideas, but for the sake of it. Some people like the game of business, just to build businesses. For me, I need a deep interest in it, or it needs to be impactful to others, and it's a slam dunk if it's both. But I hadn't done the work at the time to know all of that. It's only with journaling, programming consideration, energy pattern identification, and conscious lifestyle design, that I could start to break through, at least a little bit.

Conclusion

So first, understand the super and micro programs running you, as well as your childhood scripts, which are deeply embedded micro programs. Next, assess if the results of those programs are things you want. Then, consider how you want to live your life and what you want from it. Do that by understanding what gives you energy, fulfilment and joy, and translating it into lifestyle categories and life activities that bring about

UNDERSTANDING SOCIAL PROGRAMMING

those things. Help yourself move out of tyranny, into the desert.

PART 3

THE DESERT

ESCAPING THE PROGRAMMED WORLD

Business consultant

After leaving accountancy and failing with a recruitment business, I dabbled with e-commerce stores and started doing consulting, with the help of a mentor, to raise finance for SMEs. This was successful, and I honed a lot of communication, negotiation and presentation skills during the process. Clients were happy and started asking me to help with other work, including marketing and sales, leadership hires, and supporting key decision making, such that over time I developed into a good SME business consultant. A few years in, I was asked by a company I'd raised money for to consult as a commercial director, helping to turn the company around. This was by far the biggest project I'd ever worked on. I bought books in droves, sought the advice of mentors, and tackled the challenge head on.

It was the hardest I'd ever worked, turning up in the early hours and going home late into the night. Time was against us and I wanted to save the company, and then help it thrive. Within months, we'd amended the business model, reorganised the teams, shed a load of costs, and improved business culture and morale. The company became very profitable, and the owner asked if I'd be interested in an MBO. I was. I'd promoted a team from within, and I wanted them to be a part of it. The MBO didn't go through, and I felt extremely let down.

Digital nomad

Consequently, I decided to take time out and go travelling with my then partner. Working and studying as an accountant straight from school, I'd never had a break as an adult to just 'be'. I discovered this little website called Nomad List (not so little now!) and after some research, we decided to head to Chiang Mai. I'd recently discovered the term 'digital nomad', and fuelled by recollections of reading Tim Ferris' 4 Hour

ESCAPING THE PROGRAMMED WORLD

Workweek years earlier, it sounded like something I wanted to see.

We landed in Chiang Mai and joined a co-working space within a couple of days. So much for 'Being.' I'd recently read a Ryan Holiday blog about commonplace books, and wanted to create my own extensive one in Google Keep. This predates the 'building a second brain' craze, but the principle was the same. I shudder to think of the millions of hours lost to productivity and knowledge systems by people thinking that the activity itself equates to deep and useful work. I lost weeks to that system. Don't get me wrong, it was beautiful. But without direction in service of some larger goal, it was useless. Collecting knowledge artefacts and linking them together in the hope they might surface some useful insight, is a redundant exercise, unless you're specifically interested in the topics and have some end goal you're pursuing.

On top of the knowledge project, my partner and I were experimenting with building an online watch brand. I received a 'Daniel Wellington' watch a year earlier, and one evening got interested in how it was made, which led to the idea of making our own. Back then, Instagram was less saturated, and the idea of using it to build a product brand seemed pretty cool.

So I'm nomading in Thailand, building knowledge systems and a watch brand, and eating $1 pad thai like a millennial cliché. In the co-working space, I saw all sorts of people. There were travel bloggers living on credit cards; freelancers doing the remote work thing well, and indie hackers and startups, using the low cost of living to extend their runway and increase their chances of building a profitable business.

Enjoying the distance

I was living off savings and enjoying the distance from the world I'd left behind. That's the pertinent point, enjoying the distance, and I think it's why a lot of people decide to go and travel. Some cynics say that millennial travel culture is self-interested childishness; a generation running away from responsibility, and that wherever you go, you take you with you. Some people love the exploration of travel, and have made the intentional decision to incorporate it as part of their life plan. That's awesome. Other people are running away from their problems. But there's a third set of people, who, like myself, probably couldn't say why they'd done it, but found a sort of peaceful solitude that contrasted to the enmeshment they felt in the world they left behind.

Escaping tyranny (again)

And that's what it is, escaping tyranny again. On reflection, deep down, I didn't want to do that MBO. Sure, I was a consultant, but to all intents and purposes I was employed, working endless hours on a project, neglecting the rest of my life, for pay cheques and accolades. I liked being the boss. I liked earning money. And I liked how my Dad saw me; successful, important, in business. Ah, those pesky childhood scripts again. These weren't my desires, they were the programming I'd received from a well-meaning father, passing on his own parental and societal conditioning. And I'd been drawn into it, because left unchecked, the ego likes status and significance, it understands hierarchy, and wants to climb it. And because in the parent-child relationship, I was still a boy, desperate for his father's attention and admiration, scared to do something that might jeopardise a moment of recognition. Without introspection, we miss all that, we can't see the forces nudging us to decisions we wouldn't otherwise make. We can't see conformity with society, falling in line with the prescriptive life path laid before us; or submission to unspoken parental expectations, hoping for one more 'well done' from mum or dad.

Not all those who wander are lost

But we feel it. We sense the veneer again, the film separating us, almost severing our connection to truth and divinity and living a life in accord with who we really are. The Tolkien quote, 'not all those who wander are lost' is worth exploring in this context. For those people travelling with intention, it's true. For those people running from their problems, it's false. But here's the counter-intuitive point: for those people who travel, moving away from self-imposed tyranny at a deep subconscious level, who feel a peaceful separation when away, are less lost than those trapped in a self-imposed tyranny, who have no awareness they are so, or worse, are living with the anxious emptiness of it all.

Still in the desert

Here's the kicker, despite the temporary peace, it's still in the desert. Those that continue to wander without reading the signs, will likely feel a creeping anxiety enter into consciousness, posing questions about current worth and future plans, parental and peer judgements, and purpose and fulfilment.

The irony is that in this regard, the desert is your friend. It's whispering to you that you're out of alignment, that you haven't resolved anything except for the removal of tyranny, and that without a more fundamental change, new tyrannies will emerge once again.

It's like Neo in the matrix, trying to wake up, endlessly researching what it is, knowing it's there, even if he can't explain why, looking for ways to discover it and ultimately escape it. Not everyone is ready to leave, and when they do, it's another journey completely to arrive in paradise, without any guarantee you'll get there.

Travelling took me away from tyranny for the second time. For those first few months, the quiet solitude and observations of a different world felt like paradise. Of course, in truth, it was back into the desert. But we shouldn't fear the desert. It's a movement away from where you shouldn't be, into a space where you can figure out where to go. Consciously or not, you're collecting lessons, and at some point, you'll connect them to your foundations – the things you loved doing as a child. Or not, and you'll stay in the desert, out of the clutches of tyranny, making attempt after attempt to get back in alignment. Which is a better place to be than the tyranny you're escaping from. And with planning, structure, reflection and updates, I say you can chart a course through the desert, glimpsing paradise, for long periods at a time.

Falling into darkness

Unaware to me, I was about to fall deep into the abyss of the desert, in pitch black, without a light for guidance, paralysed and afraid. The triggering event would be the death of my dad, which was the most complicated and impactful relationship I'd had. When you lose the person you were subconsciously trying to please the most, you're left exposed, naked, alone, without direction. In truth, it took me years to climb back into the light.

LOSING MY DAD

Sick to my stomach

Travel finished in Valencia, Spain, before heading back to the UK. My sister told me we needed to get to the house the very next day, and I knew something was wrong.

Sick to my stomach, I went home. When I arrived, my parents were out, coming back from a doctor's appointment. I sat on the sofa, a child again, minuscule and scared and trying to control it with breathing. I heard the car pull up, the familiar sound of keys entering the front door lock, the opening and closing. Had I been away? Did it really happen? Was this moment real? The steps from the door to the living room, usually a moment in time, paralysed it. The interlude was awash with an overwhelming, smudged together cacophony of fears, feelings and memories.

LOSING MY DAD

Dad opened the door and saw me. 'Hello boy', he remarked. 'Hello, which one of you is it?', I managed to push out. 'Me', he said; 'Cancer, terminal'.

Terminal.

False stoic

Fuck. I couldn't help but quietly sob, trying to control the involuntary body contractions, tears leaving my eyes.

We thought we had 5 years. We barely made it through 6 weeks. He degraded so fast, and combined with breathing issues, struggled to get through the days. That crystallised when, one day, we went to call an ambulance. Dad felt panicked and begged us not to go to the hospital. But he needed help. Little did we know, he'd never leave. Something tells me he knew it was serious, and wanted to avoid it. Over the period, I was in denial, researching the illness, coming up with reasons why he had time, and remaining Stoic in my outlook. False Stoicism, if you like. Convinced I was robust to my emotions, I'd fallen into the trap of being in denial of them. Denial amplifies and pushes the problem down the road.

A 47 year dance

In the hospital, Dad got worse quickly. He had breathing troubles and an infection, and they wouldn't start chemotherapy until it had cleared up. It never did. He was swelling, in pain, starting to talk babble. Then he began bringing up bile. With this, they rushed him to emergency surgery. I arrived as they took him in. I held his hand, but couldn't bring forth words, choking on the density of it all. When opened up, they found his intestines perforated with tumours, not picked up on the scans. He almost died on the table, and was so fragile they couldn't close him up.

During the procedure, my mum, brother, sister and I were walking nearby, waiting for time to pass. In an instant, my mum dropped to the floor, howling in anguish, not knowing why, my dad's intertwined and integrated spirit leaving after a 47 year dance. When you love someone, when you're so embedded that you blur the lines between same and separate, you know in your soul when they've gone.

The funeral came and went, and we returned to emptiness. My mum would wake up daily, turn to the pillow next to her, and relive the death over and over again. Each mini-denial a sobering meeting with reality.

Pretend movement, going nowhere

And for me, stasis. I'd convinced myself to get on with life and take a couple of months to try some ideas whilst looking for a job or consulting. I went to a local coffee shop, almost daily, buying flat whites and jotting down ideas. Then I started getting anxious with it all, writing things down and researching, and writing more things down and doing more researching, but never actually getting started with anything. Pretend movement, going nowhere.

PART 3 - THE DESERT

So I decided to take a job search more seriously. Now I'm dual-tracking writing business ideas down, and logging jobs to apply for in a spreadsheet. Interwoven in my daily café ritual were little poems or journals about my life and how I was feeling, attempts from my subconscious to show me I was in pain and lost and needed to deal with it. But I wasn't ready to listen.

I took a small piece of consultancy from an old client, which helped contribute to monthly costs, but doubled as a false friend who allowed me to continue in stasis. I made progress on the job front and started doing interviews. But soon, a pattern would emerge. I'd go through rounds of talks, get offered a great position, and then decline it. At the time, I had no idea why. So then I went for lower paid jobs, wondering if I wanted something more balanced. And the same thing happened. In one instance, I accepted a well-paid, prestigious job in society's eyes, started it, showing up with intent to succeed, and lasted less than two days before quietly quitting, handing back my laptop. My reasoning at the time was that they were in such a mess, and lacking in so much information, that I had no choice but to leave. But looking back, it's clear I was in a rut, depressed, confused, pensive, surrounded by a constant air of melancholy.

The therapist saw through me

I was nudged into therapy, reluctant, annoyed at the idea, under the illusion it was for weak people who couldn't handle things. During my first session, I ducked, weaved and parried the questions, using humour to distract and deceive. Or so I thought. 'Do you always use humour as a defence mechanism?', retorted the therapist, fresh from laughing, though un-duped, contrary to my beliefs. Smack. As ex-boxer Mike Tyson said, 'everyone has a plan until they get punched in the face,' and my little game plan got ripped apart. Rendered defenceless, the therapist had in a single swing, confronted me with the truth. No more shield, I had to face it, eyeball to eyeball. In an instant, my muscle tension loosened, and I started to talk from the heart, tears and sweat outpouring as fast as my words. My feelings about dad, the complexity of loving someone complicated, his problems with cigarettes and alcohol, how he'd given up on life after losing a house and business, the impact he had on me and some of my present choices, and the unwarranted guilt I felt in the hospital, reliving the horror of confirming the switched-off life support, wondering over and over if it was the right thing to do.

The beginning of the beginning

That day crystallised the beginning of a change process. In truth, it took another 8 months before I made advancements with work, going back to consulting, and more than a year after that before making radical life changes.

Looking back, there are a couple of reasons for this. Therapy helped kickstart change, but ultimately it required courage from me to act. Courage is a muscle

LOSING MY DAD

that needs exercising, and mine was out of practice. And therapy peeled back layers, but not to the source.

I had childhood scripts running my programming, and I wasn't ready to confront them. I had awareness without understanding. I loved my dad. Growing up, I was desperate to please him, and scared to be around him, worried he'd cut me down or tell me off with words. A complete juxtaposition. He was the smartest person I've met, able to cut through noise with radical simplicity; yet he was broken, damaged from losing a family business and house, with no support group to pick him up and dust him off, haunted by a self-imposed prison of perceived failure, bitter, depressed, and hurt. He'd make a room erupt with laughter, and a second later make you feel stupid and small. He'd give you worldly wisdom, half drunk laying on the sofa. He'd tell you he's the best friend you have, and then he'd scold you for looking at the clock or answering back, or some other fabricated misdemeanour. Contrast,

contrast everywhere. And in a perverse way, as a child, it made me more desperate to please him.

The major script running my life

And so acknowledgement from my dad was one of the major scripts running my life. He'd told me I'd waste university, and pushed me into accounting, cloaking me with his own views of success, which I reluctantly followed, seeking recognition, until he moved overseas for a while, upon which I made my first break to the desert. And even post-death, I had the same script running, paralysing me with inertia, the immovable object of pleasing the father, met with the unstoppable force of the spirit telling me to take a different path. And I was repeating his patterns, albeit without cigarettes and alcohol, but stuck in a loop, a prison of my own making, a self-imposed tyranny. I wish I could tell him, "You're not broken, you're beautiful. It's not wrong to feel angst, it's your spirit telling you to take a different path, and you're more plugged in than the others, awake to it, and you need to act on it, to move into the desert, to embrace the struggle of the search for paradise."

Worse than running the same script over and over, is that I didn't know how to operate without it. Like a ghost in the shell, the script remains, neurons still covered in myelin, firing the habit pattern, needing to be replaced with something new. That's another reason for stasis. It's why we stay in tyranny. The pattern is known to us, it's serving us somehow, even if harmful. The alternative is the desert, the unknown, the void, open-ended discomfort, with no beginning and no end. When you're in stasis and you don't have answers, it's easier to stay in stasis. This is the damp reality for most of us, whether conscious of it or not.

Listen to your spirit

Without a catalyst, you may never wake up. But if you're on the wrong path, I believe your spirit is looking for ways to tell you. Whether it's angst, uncertainty, or frustration. Arguably, being encouraged to go to a therapist was my catalyst, an indication that something wasn't aligned and that I was awake to it. It's awareness. And after awareness, it's important to start moving. This is the 'out of tyranny, into the desert' moment. Movement shifts you from the known to the unknown, and as you journey, you encounter new material from which to learn, form new ideas, and develop new habit patterns. The unknown gives you new perspectives, so you can compare and contrast your historic modes of behaviour, and get new insight into why you operated the way you did. So move, bring in the new, so you can renew. Out of tyranny, into the desert.

FINDING MYSELF

Motion creates momentum

Movement surfaces new grounds for change. You might be in denial of or ignorant to fundamental things holding you back, and still make progress in the desert, as long as you're moving.

After a couple more start-stops, I ended up moving into executive search consulting, working with an established and reputable individual who showed me the ropes. My business consulting experience helped greatly. I found I could engage with business decision makers, quickly understand their business models and specific challenges, and translate that into a hiring strategy, in line with the business goals. Soon, I was doing executive search, writing reports, presenting and pitching, working with web designers, running a podcast, and building connections and community. I was flexing brain muscles, getting ideas, and developing skills. At the same time, I started journaling (mental and spiritual movement), running, and playing sports (physical movement).

Consequently, although deep in the desert, without map or compass, I was no longer stuck, wallowing in self-pity, unaware of the mental prison I'd trapped myself in. I had momentum. Additionally, I had to travel to London and used it as a way to escape a bigger life problem to solve, made real through journaling. The act of putting my thoughts on a page made louder a truth I'd been hiding from, until I summoned the courage to make a permanent life change.

A motion and solitude double-act

With a lifestyle planning framework and a healthy dose of courage, I could have done this faster. But the point is, with a motion and solitude double-act, you get the space to confirm your innermost thoughts. And you get new material and perspectives showing you possibilities for your life you didn't know could exist. With motion, you'll have been exercising your decision-making muscles, and your new experiences will have shown you that making change isn't the end of the world. And so you can act, without a compass, moving into the unknown, which I did. When you're stuck, make a change. Change your environment, change your work, change the people you meet, and seek periods of solitude. Let your inner thoughts come to the surface, sit with them, and then act.

Bigger stakes business

Through executive search and associated work, people I met began asking for business advice. I helped a guy on a management consulting project. I did a marketing consultation for a learning and development company. I worked with an entrepreneurs forum to coach the team, grow the business, and put them online and help save them when the Covid lockdowns hit. I was consulting as before, but at a higher level, serving more people, with bigger stakes involved.

As lockdowns hit, a business partner and I talked about diversifying business interests, in case our consulting dried up. We often received investment pitches, and so we decided to give them more focus. We ended up supporting a father and son EdTech start-up, first of all with advisory, and eventually in a fully-fledged time-for-equity capacity.

So, I'm now living on my own, with the world shut, doing consulting and working with the EdTech start-up. This was a period of deep work and intense self-reflection. With the start-up, over a 12 month period, we developed the business to sale to a leading UK university applications company. I brought in team members, and played a key role in masterminding the business development and ultimate sale.

Learning what you're super at

It's deep work like this that helps you learn what you're super at. I realised I have an ability to fundamentally understand how things work, know what's important,

FINDING MYSELF

make good decisions, and communicate them simply, whether verbally or in writing. Further, my enforced lockdown taught me that I like solitude, running similar routes and doing similar workouts, and doing deep work towards a specific goal, individually or with a small, empowered team. These are all great insights that I can use, moving forwards, to understand what areas I should work in, when overlaying my joy and interests, in the context of bigger lifestyle planning.

The forced environment change, and work on a new project, helped deliver this. In short, motion creates momentum, and momentum creates information, which we can use to learn more about ourselves, where we should be, and what we should be working on.

In these periods, you want to spend time in solitude, extracting your meta engagement patterns - what are you drawn to, where are your natural talents, what gives you energy? When are you happy, engaged, and in flow? What's your environment at the time? What activities are you doing? How are you interacting with other people? Is the communication asynchronous, synchronous, slow, fast, deep, or shallow?

Engagement patterns

These patterns of engagement are gold. They're materials you use to construct your ideal life. I like working on deep problems, for long stretches of time. I like periods of solitude. I like daily workouts, and running in the sun. So I need to build that into my life.

Understanding your engagement patterns - the things you're drawn to, your natural talents, what gives you energy, and what takes it away - is a key lever to design a great life and to being fully expressed as a human being.

Integrating those patterns that uplift you, and removing those that harm you, shifts how you feel, what you do, and what results you see in your life.

If you are energised by the sun but live in the cold, you're losing vitality. If you love deep conversations but

FINDING MYSELF

your work entails shallow ones, you're losing vitality. If you love interacting with people but your day is spent on your own, you're losing vitality.

Extrapolate your engagement patterns

Finally, you want to extrapolate your engagement patterns. Where else can you apply them? Is there any way to do it in things you love? I love deep work, understanding complex topics and communicating them simply, either when speaking or writing. And so I chose to write this book, about moving out of tyranny, into the desert, so you can understand who you are and how you should live, according to your being. What about you?

For me personally, this period was climbing out of the well. I hadn't found paradise, I didn't yet have the tools. But I had new material, and I had momentum, and that was enough to give me hope, to keep treading my own path, fully embracing the uncertainty of the desert.

JOURNALING FOR MY LIFE

A secret weapon

We want to live our lives the best way we can. We want to try things and build relationships and express ourselves. We have a mental image of the person we can become, fully present, and a tension when comparing this with where we are. We fail to move towards where we would like to be, getting stuck in repeating loops of committing to make change, with that change soon fizzing out, and the internal tension starting to build again. This tension shows up daily, and compounds, reaching a pouring out point where we start the loop again, or where we lock it down and internalise it, ultimately making ourselves internally twisted and unhappy and ill. Journaling is a secret weapon to recognise the loops we get stuck in, disperse pent up negative energy, and identify what we'd like to move into. Paired with other tools, such as energy pattern acknowledgement and lifestyle design, it's a super power, helping to release us from the shackles of our limiting beliefs, mental loops and societal expectations; to live a life of engagement and presence and meaning.

Spiritual intervention

Journaling saved my life. A few times now. And I'm sure it will come to my rescue again. Not in the way a surgeon rushes in and stops bleeding, putting in physical intervention after intervention to keep you alive. Instead, spiritually. Journaling has been the canvas from which I can pour out my heart, unfiltered. It's where I can list the voice in my head that's anxious, tense, frustrated or angry. It's where I can note down joy and aspirations. It's a page where I can write down all of the noise, inspect it, and patiently tease out signals I can take action on. Without it, I'd be lost, charting a course that's not my own, depressed, unhappy; frustrated that this is the narrative of my life

PART 3 - THE DESERT

and it's not how I imagined it to be as an innocent child, full of hopes and dreams.

That's the pattern most of us get into. Stuck in mental tyranny, caught in the waves, swept up into other people's wishes, pulled into the riptide, doing our best to stay above water; day after day after day. And if you feel familiar with that, at what point do you realise someone's throwing you a life jacket, if you'd just look and listen; or that there's ground underfoot, if you'd just plant your feet? If you're not open and aware and at peace inside, you don't.

And that's where journaling comes in. It's a little lifeboat that magically appears, giving you a chance to reflect and think about what you're doing. Or it's the pause button on a video game, giving you a few moments to consider your strategy and make adjustments before pressing forwards.

Journaling is useful

Journaling got me through the worst moments when my Dad was dying. It showed me that I get anxious and frustrated in stasis, and that movement is my medicine. It made me realise I'm uplifted in the sunshine, near the beach, or by the trails. It gave me perspective when I felt wronged, or served as a space to excavate negative energy from my body and confine it to the page.

I've been journaling for years. Even as a child, I'd write little poems or notes, a precursor to more detailed entries. It's an exorcism of anxiety. In a world of endless noise, it's a moment of calm, a space that creates a solitude in your mind, irrespective of where you are. It's a way to keep your character in testing times. Remarkable people throughout history used it, including the Stoic Roman Emperor Marcus Aurelius, and the courageous Jewish child in hiding, Anne Frank.

Noticing limiting patterns of behaviour

Journalling over longer periods of time can help you notice deep limiting patterns of behaviour – the negative loops you get stuck in, that stop you living a life more in line with who you are and what you enjoy.

This happened for me over the years where I lost my dad and lost my way, attempting to find it again. Journalling got me into motion, which is far better than being paralysed and unable to act. And journaling helped me understand what I'm good at, where I get energy, and what else I can apply those things to.

One day I decided to review my journals. I was in motion, but frustrated again. I felt good about the work I'd been doing and the relationship I was in, but had some internal tension that I wasn't doing deep projects in a way that lined up with my skills and interests. Checking my notes, it wasn't the first time I'd felt this way. In fact, expressed differently, the pattern was a frequently recurring one. I'd note that I want to try this new thing. Then I'd list a couple of other things I could do. Then I'd factor in making money off of it. Then I'd set out a plan to try all these things in some small way. And what happened each time, is that I'd try these things briefly, unstructured, and under the weight of trying to do them all, coupled with my existing commitments, meant they never got off the ground. At some point, something important within my existing commitments would arise, ultimately cloaking and clouding out the activities, before they were erased completely. And so I'd forget about it, internal tension building up again, until it got the better of me and I externalised it through journaling, repeating the cycle once more.

But it's in this meta-review that I caught myself. I now had my behaviour pattern, and space and time to reflect on it. With thought, I could see that:

- The act of journaling and feeling was a good thing. I was searching for alignment, and hadn't given up and blended in with the crowd.

- The occurring pattern meant it was somehow serving me. Although I didn't like it, there must be some pay-off. The pay-off was to satisfy a childhood script of not getting too involved with things. This script was limiting my life choices.

- My intention started off good, listing the new thing to try, and then got shifted, to doing things fast and looking at revenue potential. This is another childhood script – the search for success, instead of internal satisfaction.

- My worldview needed updating, so I could move past these limiting beliefs.

- In these circumstances, I tried to start too many things at once, most of which didn't truly align with who I was or what I got energy from.

- I needed a basic framework to think about what was important to me, where I felt engaged and energised, and how I should spend my time.

JOURNALING FOR MY LIFE

- I needed to do less things and do them deeply.

- I needed to lower my time preference, think longer term, slowly stack skills and experiences, and put them to use in the world.

Journaling gives you direction

Ultimately, through journaling, I thought more deeply about how to live my life, what was important to me, and how I can move towards it. Without it, I wouldn't be writing this book. And I recommend it as a tool for anyone who feels stuck, or paralysed, or frustrated; as a way to get their thoughts and feelings onto a page, in order to inspect and draw conclusions from them. I don't have a prescriptive method for how to go about it, other than to do what's more natural to you. Some people like the routine of putting thoughts to a page daily. Others like a weekly or monthly schedule. I prefer to follow my internal sense. If I feel anxiety, tension, troubled or frustrated, I journal.

PART 3 - THE DESERT

It excavates your anxiety. It helps you identify the most important task to do. It creates solitude for your mind. It brings out your patterns, both good and bad, from which you can better design a life where you feel engaged and in flow, and where you can be the best version of yourself for those around you.

Give it a try.

FINDING LOVE

She doesn't like wasting time

Before I met my wife, she'd already matter-of-factly asked me if I was looking for a serious relationship. She doesn't like wasting time. The day we were due to meet, I'd just finished a marathon all-hours business project. I was sleep-deprived and burned out, snoozing in my friend Andy's office, soaked from the rain, on the wrong side of London.

Ania texts me. "Are you still coming?" Andy took one look at a photo of Ania, asked me what my gut said, and armed with both bits of information, told me to pull my socks up and get over there.

Thank you, Andy.

PART 3 - THE DESERT

I went to a Starbucks toilet 15 minutes before the meeting; washed, dried my shirt using the dryer, did my hair, and sucked up the tiredness.

As I left Starbucks, I caught sight of Ania. She walks like her Dad. She was glancing around wondering where I was, and so I took a deep breath and approached her. She caught my eye and smiled. And she has the most beautiful smile. A smile so vivid that her eyes smile too. And in a breathless moment, I was taken in and filled up with energy and life and lightness, and I knew I was where I needed to be.

The things i fell in love with

We chatted and we clicked and we went deep quickly. And we walked and talked for 2 hours before we agreed to meet again. And walking became a staple.

And over time I'd come to learn her little idiosyncrasies, the things that make Ania Ania, the things I fell in love with. Like how she loves simple pleasures – walking to the park, buying a flat white and a cinnamon bun, and

FINDING LOVE

sitting on the bench and talking. Or peanut butter from a jar, with a spoon, nearly every day. Or that she can't eat anything without getting it on her face, ever. Or that she likes running in the rain to the point of joyful laughter.

Soul level love

It was clear our souls were dancing every time we met. A mixture of a young, fun love coupled with the wisdom of being older and knowing yourself. It's hard to know love deeply, until you know yourself. If you do know yourself, and you meet someone who knows themselves, and you're attracted to each other, and you have the same value set, you can build a special relationship together.

If you find and work on this type of love, it's really love at a soul level:

- Your values are in sync

- You're attracted to each other

- Your energy and movement patterns are in sync

- You manifest these things differently, which makes life fun

- You support each other, and help each other grow

With true love, everything is downstream of it. Love is a mirror to the importance of relationships. They are fundamental. There is no humanness without them. If you were the only human that existed in the universe, how would you know you are one? It's the relationships between things that gives them meaning.

Re-thinking lifestyle design

Love is a pull that takes you out of tyranny too. Because love takes you outside of yourself. It focuses your attention on the other. And tyranny is a prison of self. Of course, without doing the work to uncover the programming running you, you'll fall back into it, but love can be a catalyst to help set you free.

FINDING LOVE

Building a relationship with Ania got me re-thinking lifestyle design. I'd had a couple of years of work at the centre of my life, and now I needed to prioritise time invested in the relationship. Our relationship had become a key lifestyle category for us both, and so I needed to re-evaluate what was important, where to focus my time, in conjunction with Ania's goals (and later a baby). In this way, love impacts lifestyle design. You do it together. In a sense it's more restrictive, but more focused, more meaningful, and therefore more joyful.

Your partner can uncover the scripts running you

A great partner will help you uncover some of the programming running you, either through the uncovering of patterns of behaviour, or through contrasting reactions to similar experiences.

For example, we once had a small dispute that escalated. Ania said something and I reacted badly. I took myself away to reflect through writing. I realised her comment had made me feel insignificant, something that regularly happened when with my dad. And so I had reacted as my child self would have reacted, the programming activated through an emotional trigger. I told her my realisation, we quickly made amends, and now she helps me break the pattern, by lovingly calling me out on my scripts if they occur.

Love can uncover your energy patterns

Love got me thinking about energy patterns too. Ania uncovered the structure underpinning my weeks, which allowed me to be creative elsewhere. She saw I like to do the same runs and workouts, that I need movement and solitude, and that I need a project to work on. She saw those things as energy giving rather than weird. She made me comfortable in my idiosyncrasies. And I did the same for her. I saw that walks, and workouts, and healthy eating, and booking travel trips, and having time to read or go for a coffee, among other things, are all energy giving activities for her. Our love for each other helped us to identify and bring forth those activities that uplift us.

Love and family got me focused when working. It stopped me procrastinating so much. I had other lifestyle categories that were just as important – my relationship, health, and leisure – and so I knew I needed to time block and focus when doing deep work. It got me even more health focused too, because I want vitality so I can be strong and supportive to my family. I'd already focused on being physically fit, but Ania got me more dialled in with food, reducing the number of treats, making staying in good shape consistently much easier.

Family and your north star

As a family, love has given us a north star to aim for. A lifestyle design that we move towards, that we review and update, whilst upholding energy patterns, aiming for joy on a daily basis.

Choose love

A soul love allows you both to examine your self-imposed tyrannies, together, safely. You're both in the desert. By giving love, you get access to paradise, because you have a relationship and a commitment to something outside of yourself. You're not in your head all the time, it's not all about you, which is where tyranny arises. Instead, you're outside of yourself, catering to someone else, giving and receiving purely. Love helps you escape tyranny. It gives you the courage to move into the desert, and an intertwined soul to share the experience with. It's paradise, even in struggle. It's an understanding that relationship is a fundamental driver of humanness; relationship with yourself, with your loved ones, with society. Choose love.

NOW I'M A DAD

Purpose, peace, presence

Most human beings deal with an existential angst on a near daily basis. Why am I here? What's my purpose? Not everyone contemplates the questions, but most of us feel it. We feel it in our bodies, a kind of chronic tension. We see it in the weary expression on our faces, the drab hum drum of a life not fully our own, wearing us down one moment at a time. We're often stuck in our heads, replaying conversations over and over again, looking for answers, searching for a feeling where everything is aligned and we're on some kind of right path.

We want purpose, peace, and to be present. The programming forced upon us prevents this. Parental expectations, experts telling us what to do, society and media slamming down our throats how we should be and how we should act.

Unpicking the programming, finding your uplifting energy patterns, and making conscious lifestyle design choices can help you achieve this. It's what the message in this personal story is. Dealing with your scripts, understanding what makes you tick, consciously choosing a lifestyle design, navigating towards it, and removing those things that cloud it.

You know what else forces you to be present, gives you purpose, and done right, even instils in you a type of peace? A baby. Having a baby with a life partner is perhaps one of the greatest miracles you can experience, and it's a forcing function that, done right, can give you all three of these things.

Last few breaths

I'm a happy father today, however the reality is that I almost lost my wife and baby. We had a terrible birthing experience, Ania went into shock and lost a lot of blood, and little Amelie was on her last few breaths with a team of doctors and nurses quickly assisting her birth. Ania was in such a state that she hadn't realised she'd given birth, and sobbed with pure love when she awoke and saw Amelie for the first time. Nearly losing your soul mate and child sharply puts life into perspective, and makes a mockery of all the things you thought were important. I'm grateful and blessed to have them in my life, happy and healthy today.

No longer the centre of the universe

A baby fundamentally changes your life. You're no longer the centre of the universe. You probably didn't realise you were. We all think of ourselves as kind and accommodating. I did too, until having Amelie, when within a couple of weeks I realised how much time I used to have and how much of it I kept for myself, not giving, and often wasting it. But with a baby, you have a responsibility for another life. It's unconditional love. You're caring for and nurturing another life without

PART 3 - THE DESERT

expectation of reward, often at the expense of your energy, time and money.

A baby takes you outside of yourself faster than any therapy. It makes you present. In the first couple of months, you're constantly alert to any noises, or lack of noises. You exist permanently in the here and now, perhaps for the first time since you were a child yourself. It makes you fully committed to something without any expectation of reward. It completely changes your time preference, expanding your horizons, realising that good things take time to grow and evolve, and that they need love, care and nurture.

Where is the peace?

A baby can give you purpose and make you present, undoubtedly. Without effective lifestyle planning, it can be hard to establish peace. Peace isn't saying kumbaya from a mountain top, it's living a full life with responsibility from a place of serenity. Without lifestyle design, with children, you'll lose any serenity. In this sense, children are a forcing function. You're forced to consider what matters to you in your life, and how to engineer life so that those things are central. It's this juncture where lots of people give up on things, because the chaos of children stops them doing anything else, or at the very least makes a great excuse for it. You'll see friends give up on bucket list items, work goals, being healthy, or actively nourishing the relationship with their partner.

It doesn't have to be this way. In fact, children can be the catalyst to really make you think about what's important to you and your partner. 'It's great conversation material. 'Given we have kids now, what else is important to us, how do we want to live our lives, and what do we need to do to get there?' What are the categories that matter most to you both? For us, it's our family, health and fitness, our deep work projects, the right environment, and travel breaks. We talk about this regularly. It's the difference between building an engaged and joyous life with meaning and direction, versus feeling constantly overwhelmed and out of control.

Children as a forcing function

So children are a forcing function. They can either render you feeling useless, or make you extremely effective. To be effective and find serenity, you should:

- Operate as a team with designated roles. For example, I often put Amelie asleep, Ania often feeds her. Ania is responsible for everything to do with events and trips (a key life category); I'm responsible for financial decisions that move us towards our lifestyle design.

- Do active lifestyle design, be selective on the categories, and say no to noise. We choose to give time to each other, at the expense of other things. We choose to play a central role in raising Amelie. We choose deep work where we can put some of ourselves into it. We choose good health and fitness. And we choose to travel, to see overseas family, and to see new places. We try to limit distraction from this. For example, we don't own a TV, we limit social media use (although I still haven't shaken Twitter), we rarely drink alcohol, and I really look at work projects through the lens of our lifestyle design, weighing up the trade-offs before making any decisions.

- Time block your deep work and prioritise the most important things. This might be harder if you have a work commitment that requires you to be in an office all the time. If you do, look to negotiate a change where you have more flexibility and time ownership, unless your lifestyle design is such that you want to be in an office at designated hours. I aim to do my deep work in the morning, and then do any calls or emails in the early afternoon, with time to look after Amelie, take a walk, and work out. This isn't prescriptive, but the practice forces me to consciously think about how I can be effective,

PART 3 - THE DESERT

and how to give time to all areas within our lifestyle design.

- Respect your energy patterns. I need movement, solitude and less frequent but more in depth communication. I get energy interacting with and impacting individual and small groups of people, but lose energy interacting in big groups. What are your energy patterns? How can you build them into your life? The more energy giving patterns you have, the more you can give to your life categories, the more serenity you have.

- Make time for your partner. My wife feels love when she has quality time with me. Time is important to her. It's a space for us to connect and nourish our relationship. So many couples lose their connection because they haven't made adequate time to consciously choose each other. A common rebuttal is to say there's no time for that. But at what cost? At the cost of your relationship, your happiness, your peace? With lifestyle design, if it's important to you, you realise you must make time for it.

Children and choosing the life you want

And so, children put actively choosing the life you want to the front and centre. With a child, you get purpose and presence. Add in lifestyle design, and you get peace. You become effective, you do things that contribute to your shared vision, you activate energy patterns that uplift you, which will ultimately make you a better parent.

With love and lifestyle design, a baby can take you out of tyranny. Nurturing life is a form of paradise. It's the highest privilege. Propagating your combined genes and trying to give your offspring better material than you had, can give you a life of meaning where there may have been a void. And nurturing life gives you a new perspective about what's important. It gives you orientation and direction. For me, it was a forcing function. It took me further from any self-imposed

PART 3 - THE DESERT

tyrannies. It gives meaning to the desert. And it's its own form of paradise.

A PIECE OF YOUR SOUL IN ALL THINGS

Hi ren

I found a music video on YouTube called 'Hi Ren', made by an independent artist of the same name. The performance really grabbed me. There was a cool guitar intro, amazing singing, rapping, incredible lyrics, and clever symbolism. These qualities are present in a number of songs, but this one had me playing it on repeat, listening intently, unpicking the story, looking for little meanings. In fact, the first few times I watched it, I was hot, sweaty, fully engaged, fully present, tears in my eyes, pulled into the song, captured by the raw humanness of it. Other songs have similar qualities, but don't hit me in nearly the same way. Why is that? Because this video was about the artist, a duel between the light and dark in his mind, a performance uncovering tyranny, doubt, imposter syndrome and hope; a story of his past and the demons he'd overcome. You can see in the performance it's a song from the heart, and you can read in the comments how the viewers feel seen. By putting himself into his art, Ren was self-expressed, undertaking the act of overcoming personal tyranny, and connecting with and impacting people who see themselves in it and feel the same way.

Longing for meaning

In our lives, most of us long for meaning, for some kind of higher purpose, to matter. But then we follow the lines of society and fall into mechanical ways, replacing thought with formality and dreams with deadlines. And we start to feel anxious and tense and empty at the robotic nature of our existence. Or we get burned out. Or worse, we numb ourselves and turn off our humanness, preferring to live on someone else's programming than to feel all sorts of uncomfortable. It doesn't need to be this way. We can achieve meaning by putting a piece of ourselves in all we do, whether it's our work, our hobbies, our health, or our relationships. We can externalise the internal and move from self-obsession to self-expression, engaging fully with life, authentically, feeling more aligned and connected to it, and aligning and connecting more with the relationships around us. Like Ren did in his music video, we can do in our lives.

Vivid dread

I remember with a kind of vivid dread working in an accountancy practice. My Dad told me to move into it, thinking it would one day get me into investment banking or private equity somehow, like those tracks were the correct aspirations to have. Panicked stasis became normal for me. Every day at work I'd feel anxious, my heart rate up, chest pounding, skin crawling, necking coffee after coffee to get through the day. And at some point I tried to numb it out. I earned well, and was on a path to a great position in the company. I assumed this is what life was, and that I'd grow out of feeling sick. This is a version of behaving mechanically. A copy of a copy, running a similar program to thousands of other people across the world. This path can often end in breakdown, burnout, or worse, numbness to your soul, numbness to the things that light you up and give you joy, trading it all for a bigger paycheck and better shoes. In this way, we lose sight of personal meaning and end up attaching it to better status or bigger bank balances.

Get your meaning back

You can get your personal meaning back by putting yourself into the things that you do. By imbuing a piece of yourself into the things you touch, you're interacting with the world rather than just existing in it. You can feel that, and so can other people. It doesn't have to be as grand as the music video by Ren. It's doing a sport and playing your own style, rather than the prescriptive best-fit style taught to you. It's taking on a work project and adding craft and additions of your own, instead of routinely going through the templates. It's doing your hobby and sharing it with the world for the joy of it. It's writing blog posts and social media updates from experience and authenticity, rather than with mechanised hooks and clickbait. It's engaging with your partner and being one hundred percent you, not pretending to be someone else, just connecting and relating. It's this book. It's the little interactions and the big things too; like consciously considering your life and your energy patterns. Doing these things is putting yourself into the design of your life at the highest level. And it makes putting your soul into things easier, because you've designed for those things in the first place.

Being human

Putting a piece of yourself in the things you do is human. The modern world confuses this, often optimising to replace human uniqueness. And a lot of the conveniences are great. For example, I love working in a Starbucks, and I'm grateful aeroplanes follow standardised checklist procedures. But it's our humanness that creates connection between each other. And it's depth of connection that builds relationships, and it's our relationships that underpin everything else.

Self-expression

You feel it when you're being self-expressed. Children do it automatically. It's flow, joy, engagement, love. And other people feel it too. The act of being you, being present, saying no to the programming, and letting the shining light of your humanness come forth, is a courageous act. It puts you in alignment with your being, and it's inspiring to others because they can feel your authenticity and humanness, they can see you dripping with aliveness. In my consulting, there was this one time I interviewed a lady called Rina. From the moment we talked, Rina radiated truth. She spoke with beauty in her words, and cut straight to connection. She ignored the rote answers and the business language, and instead gave the best thing she possibly could have done; herself, truthfully. Rina had a successful career, built through skill and experience, and also built

A PIECE OF YOUR SOUL IN ALL THINGS

through the creation and maintenance of incredible relationships. People saw she was putting herself fully into her interactions and her work, and they wanted to be a part of it. Her authenticity was inspiring.

A piece of your soul in all things is rejecting the standard scripts and programming of life, tearing up the hymn sheet and writing your own verses. It's forgetting status and outcomes and focusing on presence and truth. It's taking you from angst and self-obsession to doing something that impacts others through self-expression. It's a better way to live for you because you're in alignment, engaged with life and full of vitality. And instead of the paralysis and fear that comes with searching for meaning, you're making meaning on a daily basis, through the way that you live, the work you do, and how you interact with others.

Try it on, drop the charades, see how you like it.

FAITH IN A HIGHER POWER

Something greater than you

We want to be in alignment with our being, to have the courage to step into the unknown, into the desert, trusting the journey, seeking a mental, physical and spiritual paradise as we go about it.

But we get trapped in the tyranny of our minds, our clever logic, self-imposed mental prisons, and reinforced societal, parental and 'expert' programming. We become self-obsessed, anxious, stuck in mental loops that paralyse us and stop us from starting. Or we fall into a stasis, deadening ourselves inside, desperately ignoring any internal signal that something's wrong, that we're not being as we should be, as we each uniquely are.

FAITH IN A HIGHER POWER

What we need is faith in a higher power. You might call it God, Allah, Brahman, the Universe, The Way, Mother Earth, or a Higher Consciousness. Faith in a higher power is surrender to fate, an acknowledgement that some events cannot be seen, and that you're not in control of them. Faith is letting something greater than you into your heart to guide you, giving you courage to take action, with perspective, over the long term, in accordance with a higher standard.

Faith takes you out of the mental prison of your mind and into the expansiveness and richness of the world. It takes us out of tyranny, into the desert, guided, at peace, in joy, taking steps towards paradise.

Lost with no compass

When I'd taken my first steps into the desert, leaving accountancy, I set up a recruitment business with a friend. We made a great start, until my friend suffered some personal problems and quickly went off the rails. Without him, at that stage, I didn't feel confident to

PART 3 - THE DESERT

continue. Lacking a compass, I struggled to know what to do. I lived in a tiny flat, with my savings dwindling, and anxiety flowing through my veins. As time passed, neuroticism took hold, and the devil entered my mind. 'I'm a failure,' 'I left an accelerating career for this', 'what will my Dad think of me?' I remember one particular day, staring at my living room walls, letting out a roar of frustration. It's agony to be paralysed by indecision and not knowing. Your brain races, surfacing thought after thought after thought; a mixture of ideas, fears, and self-oppression; a concoction that creates a permanent panic undercurrent, residing with you wherever you go. The thought overload jams any signal and forces you into a frenzied stasis, unable to take action on anything, exhausted at not being able to. We tie ourselves in knots, searching for an answer now, as if it's a bounded problem with a perfect solution, and we're stupid for not finding it.

My Dad suffered the same, on a larger scale. He lost his family business and house in quick succession, and fell into a punch drunk pit of despair, manifesting itself as a defeated, depressed lethargy. With the wrong friend group and no code to turn to, his scripts took over so strongly that punch drunk turned to drunk, with addiction and depression ruling the next 25 years of his existence. One of the smartest people I've met, his intelligence built a mental tyrannical prison with strong bars and high walls. He tortured himself to the grave.

It doesn't have to be this way, but it is for so many of us to varying degrees.

My wife and faith

My wife has always believed in God. From a young age, she went to church, and throughout adulthood, she's joined various Christian groups, looking for different perspectives. Her friends know her as lucky. The running joke is that things seem to work out for her, no matter what situation she finds herself in. I've witnessed it myself, even at a silly scale. She'll leave a jacket at the airport and it will be there when she returns. She'll drop

PART 3 - THE DESERT

her credit card only to have someone return it to her at the exact moment she goes back for it. She'll take last minute trips with a passport and rucksack, and luck will seem to work out for her.

If you ask her why she's lucky, she'll probably tell you faith, prayer, ritual and intention. The examples above may seem silly, a hot hand, a lucky streak, a statistical anomaly. And so then she may tell you that, lost in the desert herself one day, after leaving a church group, she turned to God and prayed for guidance. She parked her intellect and put her faith in a higher power. And she felt God in her heart and was compelled to enter a new stage of her life, to find a soul mate. When she had accepted this, and felt ready, she did a rosary prayer that was to be repeated for 54 days, asking for guidance and to be introduced to her soul mate. And on the 55th day, the day after the prayer finished, she met me for the first time. I love this story. Being human, it makes me swell up inside a little. But more importantly, I believe in my heart that we're soul mates, that we were both searching for each other, and that our spirits intertwined at the exact moment they were supposed to. And she manifested this firstly by putting her faith in a higher power.

Surrender and perspective

Faith in a higher power can be a guiding light and comforting hand in times of difficulty. I fell back into tyranny, and my Dad never left it, because we became slaves in a mental prison that we'd made for ourselves. My 'failure' was driving me mad, and I was trying to construct an answer in the very moment of my neurosis. And yet we know that answers generally come to us in moments of stillness, when the buzz of the mind is quietened; for example, in the shower, taking a walk, playing a sport, or in prayer.

Faith in a higher power – whether you call it God, The Way, The Universe, Brahman, Allah, or a Higher Consciousness – takes you out of your head and surrenders you to accept that you aren't God and you can't know everything, that some things are vastly more complex than you can comprehend; and that right intention, faith, and action is the best medicine we can take to navigate this reality.

It gives us perspective. We're just one being in a sea of beings, doing our best, attempting to give a good account of ourselves, for the brief amount of time we have. It gives us a set of rituals and moral code to follow at all times, and is particularly useful in times of uncertainty. It keeps us away, or pulls us back from vice and temptation. It's a torch to help us find our way out of addiction. It's a spiritual elixir that fills us with the courage to act on our convictions. We can outsource our doubt to the universe and let faith guide us instead. It gives us peace, calm, and stillness. It makes us think longer term, and stops us from cheating ourselves with short term gains that will hurt us down the road.

FAITH IN A HIGHER POWER

Action and momentum

I asked my wife why she has faith in God. She told me that she can see his power in her life, that she can feel him in her heart, guiding her with decisions, and that prayer gives her peace. My wife is excellent at taking action, and consequently, she has a richness to her life because of the numerous experiences she's had. Rather than be paralysed by her metal prison, she places her courage and faith in God, and takes action with this strength. In this way, faith creates momentum. It's a pull to life, to vitality.

Faith takes you out of tyranny, into the desert, with strength, courage, and love. Had I had faith in a higher power when lost after the failure of my first venture, I could have placed trust in the process, and been open to experiences, and the momentum would have opened up new opportunities much faster than the way things played out.

Had my Dad had faith in something bigger, a code to follow in times of despair, a compass to guide him out of the darkness, he may have had a shot at escaping his mental prison. He may have regained the light that resided inside him which burned for far too short a time.

Be open to a higher power

I often attend church with my wife on a Sunday. It's a modern version, with a cool band, and an eloquent pastor who creates relevant sermons applicable to everyday life. I sometimes disagree with parts of the sermon, and talk with my wife about it after the service. One particular day, the sermon was about faith. I disagreed with the message. Kindly, my wife looked deep into my eyes, and told me that my desire to want to solve everything myself was probably the biggest force in my life so far, and yet the biggest constraint to me being more powerful in my being, to accessing love and joy in a deeper and more connected way. She said that I'd feel more, do more, experience more, if I put my trust in God when I went about my days, when I

FAITH IN A HIGHER POWER

undertook projects, and when I considered the vision for my life, for our life.

And she's right. Faith in a higher power can get me out of the tyranny of my own mind. It can transform overwhelm and uncertainty to love, courage, action and momentum. It changes the 'should haves' into the 'dids' – "I should have written that book" became "I wrote a book about moving away from tyranny, into the desert, in search of paradise; by overcoming your childhood scripts, auditing your past to find the things that light you up, undertaking conscious lifestyle design, and placing your faith in a higher power that things will work out."

Whatever you call it, have faith in a higher power.

WHAT'S ESSENTIAL IS INVISIBLE TO THE EYE

What's important to us

The most important things in life are mostly unseen. They aren't material things, money or status, They're the hidden things, like friendships, love, health, meaning and giving.

A lot of the tyranny we go through in life is the forgetting of what's important to us, these things that we naturally value; and instead chasing things unimportant to us, things we're told to value.

When we're young; we play, we add meaning, we love, we practise, we tell stories, we see beauty. Then we're told what to do, what to think, how to feel. And as adults, we chase money, job titles, and consumption. We stop practising and loving, we forget about the

WHAT'S ESSENTIAL IS INVISIBLE TO THE EYE

stories, and lose all sense of meaning. We forget what we knew instinctively.

The little prince - how we forget what's important

The famous book 'The Little Prince' tells this story well. In the story, the Little Prince needs to find his way home, and during his journey, meets a number of characters – the king, the conceited man, the drunk, the businessman, the lamplighter, and the geographer. Each of the characters is ruled by some tyranny, and has lost sight of the little things that add humanness to life. The king wants absolute power, to rule for the sake of ruling. The conceited man wants admirers, he wants to be told how special he is, irrespective of what he does. The drunk has lost his way to the bottle. The businessman is busy counting. He wants to own everything, but hasn't really questioned why. The lamplighter constantly lights lamps. He's a busy work fool, forgetting to ask what he's living for and what would bring him joy. And the geographer documents and makes maps of things, without visiting, exploring or experiencing them himself. He mistakes second-hand experience for first-hand living. All of the characters represent the ways we end up living the lives we're told to live, forgetting what we truly love. In different forms, they scoff at friendship, love, beauty and play, citing them as unimportant. When we strip it back, these are the things we live for, and yet along the way we swap them for a bigger paycheck, or more applause, or increased power, or safe monotony, or irresponsibility.

The fox - the importance of understanding

Later in the book, the Little Prince meets a fox, and wants to befriend and play with him. The fox responds that he needs to be tamed before he can become a friend to the Little Prince. The fox was asking the Little Prince to invest time into him, to be patient, to understand him. He said that people have no time to understand anything, that they want to buy everything ready made. But there are no shops where you can buy friendships.

It's your relationship to people and things that give them meaning to you. Without the Little Prince taming the fox, it's just a fox like 1,000 others. But by taming the fox, by building a relationship with it, the fox becomes unique to the Little Prince in all the world.

This is a key insight to a life of breakthrough living, for escaping tyranny and moving into the desert, enjoying moments of paradise. It's your relationship to things that gives them meaning to you. And it's a sense of meaning that gives fulfilment to your life. It's a lack of meaning that makes life empty. When you're living by the scripts of other people – your parents, societal conditioning, your peers – and when you pursue what you're told is important – money, status, prestige – without regard to personal meaning and self-expression, you fall into anxiety, stasis and upset.

Upon their goodbyes, the fox tells the Little Prince his secret:

"It is only with the heart that one can see rightly; what is essential is invisible to the eye."

The rose - relationship and responsibility

The fox goes on to talk about a rose the Little Prince cares for on his home planet. Before meeting the fox, the Little Prince had walked into a field of roses, and felt sad that his rose wasn't unique, that it was the same as all the roses he was walking between.

And here's the foxes point: it's the time the Little Prince has spent building a relationship with his rose, that makes his rose so important. To the eye, a rose is a rose. To the heart, the Little Prince's rose is the most important thing in the world. And through taming her, through relationship with her, he becomes responsible for her. And it's through relationship and responsibility that he finds deep meaning.

Creating a breakthrough life

It's through relationships and responsibility that we can cultivate a breakthrough life. Relationship and responsibil-ity to people, relationship and responsibility to things, relationship and responsibility to ourselves.

With lifestyle design, you're understanding what you value. This is the externalisation of what's inside your heart. You're taking responsibility for the things that give you meaning. To increase the meaning they give you, you focus on building relationships with those things. This expands beyond people. If you care about your health, and you prioritise it, then you take time to understand it and improve it. In essence, you're taming it, getting to know it, building a relationship with it. If you want to be a writer, learn guitar, or build an app; it's the same thing. You can't do it well, unless you take time to tame the subject matter, to understand it, get intimate with it and relate to it. All good comes from

PART 3 - THE DESERT

relationship and responsibility, from the invisible, from the unseen.

Relationship and responsibility in my life

I see this reflected in my own life. My tyranny evolved from living a life that wasn't my own, without knowing it. I followed the scripts of my father, and the programming from society. I struggled for meaning because I couldn't relate to the subject matter; a career in accountancy and the status and prestige of Partnership. Breaking free of tyranny, moving from the known to the unknown, set me upon a journey to find meaning. It took years to fully understand that meaning arises from relationship and responsibility, and that we can find those things we're drawn to through the identification of positive energy patterns and lifestyle design.

I see it in my relationships. I love my wife, my daughter, my family and close friends in part because of a natural pull to them, and in part because of the time spent to understand them, relate to them, support them and grow with them.

I see it in my health and fitness. With time and effort, I've come to understand my body, and my engagement with and use of it has given me meaning in my relationship with it.

And I see it in my work. For years I'd learn a little of something and move on, cultivating 'options'. But writing remained one of the staples. Through focus, through building my relationship with writing; through practice; I've developed meaning in the exercise, to the point where it has become a tool of self-expression for me. And if I choose to do something else, I understand that I need to work at it, build skills, take time with it, engage with it, and relate to it, for it to have meaning for me and for me to be meaningful with it.

Our deep relationships with people and things, and responsibility for them, gives us meaning and makes them unique to us because, in effect, we are embedding ourselves into them. We are giving a piece of ourselves to them, which changes them, changes us, and changes the relationship between both.

What's essential is invisible to the eye.

PART 4
LESSONS LEARNED

TO DO PUSH-UPS, DO PUSH-UPS

Radical simplicity

Sometimes radical simplicity can produce more effective results than optimised plans.

Take working out to build fitness, strength and to lead a healthy life. In years gone by, I've done detailed gym workouts, drunk protein shakes, bought a running watch, bought information products, and watched Youtube videos. I've been varying weights and sizes.

But as I've gotten older, I've found that the fitness that works best is the thing I stick to with consistency. And for me, sticking to something means reducing the friction to do it. Reducing friction means the activity should be accessible, I should be engaged, and at best, having fun.

TO DO PUSH-UPS, DO PUSH-UPS

Unless doing weights is the thing I want to do deep work on, obsessively planning workouts, buying gadgets, and logging entries in a spreadsheet are all friction creating activities.

I've done them all before, forcing myself to create records, until I run out of willpower to continue tracking so extensively, draining myself of the vitality to give my best in the activity.

What's your why?

Too much meta activity can diminish the activity itself.

Instead, figure out why you're doing the activity in the first place. I'm working out for longevity and to feel good. I want my body to be strong, adapted to the world, free of disease, strong enough to fight gravity, so I can enjoy life and stay active well into old age. I watched my Dad die at 62, body ravaged from too much beer and wine and too many cigarettes.

Then I work out and run to complement playing squash, going on hikes with my wife, and effortlessly carrying my daughter up and down the stairs. Finally, I work out because I enjoy it. I enjoy pushing myself, ridding my mind of noise, forced into flow and engagement with the present moment.

With my north star in mind, I'm comfortable not tracking every metric just because some guru is telling me to do so. Instead, my view is, what are the key variables, which mean I don't need to look at others?

Simple, repeatable, direct

And so I do really simple workouts, with really simple metrics. I do push ups, pull ups, squats, lunges, dips, and a few other variations.

One day in the week, I'll set a minimum number of press-ups to do, and I'll do them. I'll do them in the maximum number of reps I can per set, to build strength, done in an arbitrary amount of time; say 20 minutes. This gives me time to recover between sets,

TO DO PUSH-UPS, DO PUSH-UPS

but only just, so I'm working hard consistently. Now, I can tell I'm getting stronger, if the maximum reps per set increases, if the average number of reps per set increases, and if the total reps in a given time period increases. If I get strong enough, I'll buy a weight vest, to make the task harder.

I'll do the same with the other activities. Gym bros might read this and tell me it's not optimal. And they're right. It's not optimal, but it's good. And it's repeatable. And there are no barriers to entry. And with a couple of numbers and a mirror, I can see progress. Coupled with other health and fitness work, like diet, runs, sprints, walks, and sport, it's a longevity and feel good amplifier.

And it's straight to the heart of the task. No complicated programs, no expensive memberships, no gadgets. Just push-ups. By going straight to the activity, you remove all of the weight surrounding it, and get instant feedback from it. It's learning from doing, growing from doing, being from doing.

PART 4 - LESSONS LEARNED

Can't do push-ups? Then do reverse push-ups (go down slowly), or push-ups from your knees. Build up until you can do one. That's your 'smashing through the glass ceiling' moment. It's rewarding. It's instant feedback. You're gaining momentum, building your body, strengthening your mind, and opening your being up to what's possible for you. All from doing push-ups, rather than all the activities that surround the push-ups.

And so if you want to do push-ups, do push-ups.

This chapter isn't just about push-ups.

DEPTH IS GREATER THAN BREADTH

Depth is greater than breadth

For a fulfilling life, depth is greater than breadth. You should figure out where you want to focus your time and spend it there, saying no to most other things. By going deep on something, you end up learning lots of other skills because you can relate them to your deep topic of interest. Going deep, rather than broad, is applicable to your health, work, and relationships.

Options

Some prevailing wisdom says to collect options, increasing your luck surface area. Options without roots are like leaves in the wind, blowing aimlessly. Options rooted to something is like a tree seeking sunlight, stretching in new directions, growing, whilst continually nourishing its core.

PART 4 - LESSONS LEARNED

If you increase your time horizon, depth can create rooted options, and increase your luck surface area. Depth increases insights, learnings, connections, and eventually, opportunities. It's taken me years to appreciate this. I'm only really living it right now.

And a few hours of deep work, on a specific task, pushing your skills to the limit, will be more interesting and engaging than shallow work. It's deliberate practice.

Martial artist Bruce Lee said, 'I don't fear the man who has practised 10,000 different kicks. I fear the man who has practised one kick 10,000 times.'

The interconnectedness of everything

One single setting can hold the keys to the universe. It's depth that opens up the interconnectedness of everything. Take Bitcoin. At a high level, it's digitally sound money. You can save with it, you can spend it. There are only so many, and no one can devalue yours by printing more. You don't need a bank to store them.

DEPTH IS GREATER THAN BREADTH

This is enough to make you consider owning some. But if you are really interested in it, you might end up learning about: the history of money, cryptography, hashing algorithms, Austrian economics, psychology, game theory, systems thinking, time preference and much, much more. The deeper you go into it, the more you'll learn about the world, the more you'll learn about yourself, and the more you'll change in relation to your updated integrated insights and perspectives.

And this is why depth is greater than breadth, because going deep engages you, educates you, and updates you. Breadth doesn't have the same power.

Depth in action

Let's look at some examples.

Take health and fitness. You can get caught up on the latest gadgets, measuring everything. You can join gyms and classes. Lift tens of different weights, constantly update your program, doing a little bit of everything. Or you can pick one thing, like callisthenics

PART 4 - LESSONS LEARNED

and just practise the foundations over and over, building strength and knowledge about your body.

Or take relationships. You get more from a few deep, engaged relationships, than you do thousands of digital friends. I can talk to my best friend about anything and everything. Our mental models of each other are continually updating, and so we engage more fluidly than when meeting people for the first time. We're not transacting, either. We're in conversation for the conversation. Dancing for the dance, which is more wholesome and human and lovely, and leaves you feeling good. Contrast that with Twitter arguments, or Linkedin virtue signalling; where you become a twisted, weakened version of yourself, fitting an algorithmic box.

You can expand the reasoning beyond deep friendships, to deep intellectual, creative, or other relationships. The argument goes that Twitter or similar can be an intellectual salon, and you'll miss out not engaging there. But imagine the hours lost to Twitter, impacting the ability to go deep anywhere. Better to scale back your shallow effort, and instead arrange specific deep conversations with people where you'll get genuine life changing output, that can lead to insight, exploration and opportunities.

It's the same reasoning with your life partner. What's deeper, having single serving relations with a multitude of people, a brief lustful embrace and meek exit; or to build a life with someone your love, learning with and updating each other, nourishing each other, encouraging each other, bringing life into the world, making memories and sharing stories?

Depth increases your time horizon

Depth increases your time horizon. It makes you see life as craft, or art, and you the craftsperson, or artist. It makes you a self author, writing and continually updating your own life book.

In the context of life planning, depth makes you look at life holistically, build it around those things that matter

PART 4 - LESSONS LEARNED

to you, and orient it to spend as much time as possible doing those things.

For example, you might decide you want to go deep on your relationships with your partner and children (if you have them), a sport, and your deep work (for example, a Youtube fitness channel); in a sunny and vibrant environment. So you prioritise living in the appropriate location, carving our focus time for your family, cutting back on sugar and seed oils, and doing four hours deep work on your channel every day. You say no to options outside of your chosen life, or at the very least, you weigh them very carefully against what you'd have to give up to pursue them. With your channel, over time, you end up learning a variety of fitness workouts, videography, lighting, video editing, Youtube analytics, publishing, and more.

Go deep enough, and you end up building out foundations across a number of disciplines, with the huge advantage that you know them better, because they have roots that tie to your principal interest, and

DEPTH IS GREATER THAN BREADTH

so you understand the inter-relationships between them.

Consult your heart

So, depth is greater than breadth. The internet makes you think you're missing out, all the time. You get cheap dopamine hits taking you from one prescriptive idea to the next. Before you know it, years have gone by, and you have an ever growing list of things you've started and left, and things you want to try. Of these, some will be things emanating from other people, that you think you should do, because of the human preponderance for mimicry. The rest will be things you really do want to do, but keep putting them off, because of some incorrect measure of what's important. Instead, you should consult your heart, think about the things you love doing, tease out the meta-skills and behaviours, choose key things to do in service of a life plan, and get started.

DOING IS LEARNING

Are you focused, anon?

My wife has a useful ignorance about her which is spellbindingly beautiful. Let me explain. When I have a new project idea, my natural proclivity is to try and think about all the moving parts. Take writing a book. I might get the initial book idea with an intense enthusiasm. Shortly after, I'll start thinking about writing software. Then I might think about pre-book audience building, a content plan, print-on-demand and e-books, amazon ads and marketing. Now I'm off the core idea, the book, and onto an imagined future of complex moving parts. So I'll probably buy books and watch Youtube videos on each of these things, scribbling notes, updating my mental model of how things work and what needs to be done. And I'll do this on and off for a few months,

DOING IS LEARNING

coming back to it, promising myself I'll get started as soon as I finish the latest bit of research.

What started as a beautiful, pure, inspiration-driven idea; morphed into a mental paralysis prison.

And in this regard, knowledge is a dangerous thing! In the example, I never even started writing. And it's a real example. I promised myself for years I'd write books, journaling and joking with my family about it. And I'm guessing lots of you reading this can relate. Go have a look at your project ideas folder or to do list. How far back do the entries go? When are you going to start it?

To start a youtube channel, record a video

Contrast this with my wife. Years ago, she did fitness instructor qualifications and dance choreography. She's always worked out, religiously. And she's super health conscious. Which is to say, health and fitness forms a cornerstone of her life. After giving birth to our daughter, she got back in shape within 3 months,

PART 4 - LESSONS LEARNED

mesmerising her friends and family. And as time passed, we decided for her not to return to work, so we can both focus on raising our daughter. As such, she wanted to undertake a new project, and had an idea for a fitness workouts Youtube channel.

When she told me the idea, I was stoked. Instantly, my mind raced. I started talking about cameras, lighting, video editing software and Youtube analytics. My wife smiled at me, not knowing any of these things, and I went to bed resolute, thinking I needed to help her scope it out. The next day, fresh from a run, I went to my home office, where I found my wife working out, recording a video, using her camera phone and a tripod. Which is to say, she was doing the precise thing she talked about. No bullshit, just straight on the task.

Constant small improvements

She played the video back, and soon got downbeat with the image quality. So she looked into her phone settings, switched from high definition to 4k, and pressed record again. Reviewing the footage, she saw an improvement, and was happy. So she did more. In fact, over a couple of weeks, she did tens more, tinkering with the settings, tripod placement, and time of day recording to take advantage of the natural light.

Then one evening I came to bed, and she's on her laptop, frustrated. She tells me she needed to edit the video, Googled a software, paid a load of money, and found it to be glitchy and difficult to use. So she got a refund and tried another one. Before I know it, she's edited the video, removed audio, and added in timers. Then she's looking at how to get the workout audio files and overlay them. Days later, she tells me she's going to finish this set of videos in the software, but will need to learn a better one if she ever wants to produce a video of the quality of some bigger channels.

Next, she's on Youtube, having never used it as a creator before, uploading and preparing the videos. Then she finds out she needs thumbnails, and after a quick Google search, finds a software to create them in. I asked her if she'd given thought to video titles, mentioning keyword and analytics softwares. She didn't know they existed, so instead, she'd searched her favourite channels, making notes on the video titles, video lengths, and views. Software can come later. Before I know it, she's created, edited, and published ten videos.

Useful ignorance

And so, useful ignorance plus intention is a super power. There's me scoping out projects, researching, using my knowledge to grind me to a halt before I've begun. And there's my wife, going straight to the main task, and then overcoming the bottlenecks as she encounters them, building skills along the way.

The key differentiator, is in my example, by researching, I have the illusion of knowledge, but never actually create something. In my wife's example, she has knowledge ignorance, and so creates something by doing, learning as a by-product of her work.

Doing is learning

And therefore, doing is learning. It's the fastest way to learn. My wife went from nothing to publishing videos in no time at all, by going to the heart of the craft, and struggling at the limit of her ability, slowly expanding it. At the time of writing, she still doesn't have a large knowledge of the various skills that go into making a great channel, and will have lots to learn. But she's gone straight to doing, and has practised the basics over and over again. This means two things. First, by diving in with useful ignorance, she's tightened the feedback loop between doing something and seeing the results, because she needs positive results to be able to resume her craft. Second, she's building out the skills required to do the craft, in a way that's tightly coupled with the craft itself. In this way, she's learning the skills much more deeply than just learning them in isolation, hoping to one day put them into practice.

PART 4 - LESSONS LEARNED

In a previous chapter, I wrote about depth being greater than depth, and you can see it in action here. Coupled with this insight, we have a superpower:

- Depth is greater than breadth

- Doing is greater than learning

So, choose those things you want to get into, in the context of a larger life plan, and dive into them, like a hero on an adventure, overcoming obstacles as you encounter them. It's the fastest way to learning, depth, and fulfilment, and will be a significant contributor to living a good life.

REMOVE 90% OF EVERYTHING

Free up space and time

Remove things that harm you. Remove things negatively affecting your body, mental and spiritual health.

Remove toxic relationships, self-serving 'friends', and judgemental colleagues. Remove alcohol, drugs, cigarettes and sugar. Remove the temptations from your house. Clear your cupboards of cakes, biscuits, beer, seed oils, margarine, pastries and crisps. Make these things the exception, not the rule.

Remove the need to have to think about these things. Remove them completely. Don't make them a part of your day to day world. Engage them on your terms only.

PART 4 - LESSONS LEARNED

Remove things that cost you. Remove things impacting your bank account, your ability to save, the ability to buy back your time. Remove expensive houses and keeping up with the Jones. Remove car payments, the latest flashy technology gadgets, TV packages, excess subscriptions and unused memberships.

Remove the things that cost you without serving you. Create space to breathe, think clearly, save and compound.

Remove things that clutter you. Remove bloat. Get rid of clothes you haven't worn in a year. Gift the books collecting dust on your shelves. Sell the six phones and two laptops sitting in your drawers. Clear out the old golf clubs, football boots, and spare toaster. Free up space, leaving those things you genuinely get value from.

Remove work that doesn't serve large goals. Remove meetings, slack messages, powerpoint presentations and daily commutes. Remove weekly check-ins and

REMOVE 90% OF EVERYTHING

schmoozing. Remove your job if it doesn't serve your greater life plan. Do just those things that are deep work, moving you towards completing a valuable project, where you learn skills and gain knowledge, in flow, integrating into your own continual human development.

Remove complicated diet and fitness plans. Remove points charts and step counters. Remove multi-thousand dollar equipment. Remove your list of 35 gurus. Prioritise movement, compound exercises, eating a protein-dominant whole foods diet, and having fun.

Remove complexity in your business. Remove 30-step sales and marketing funnels. Remove the pool of freelancers. Remove meetings. Remove the five things you're trying to be that aren't part of your core product or service. Remove complicated checkout funnels and clickbait posts. Remove everything that isn't a priority for your customer. Leave yourself with a truly valuable

PART 4 - LESSONS LEARNED

product or service, with a simple way to get in front of customers, and a simple way to deliver the value.

Remove constant connection from your life. Remove your phone from your hand. Remove Tiktok, Snapchat, Twitter and others. Remove Slack notifications. Unsubscribe from all newsletters except those that nourish you. Remove an open calendar, or the ability to be contacted all hours of the day (except from core family or friends). Remove the empty dopamine hits, syphoning away your attention and your ability to concentrate. Leave those connections that serve you, deeply, and will continue to do so for years to come.

Life will be ten times more peaceful when you do these things, bringing a sense of calm, quietude, and belonging. You'll have time, your most important asset, and separation, to think deeply about what's useful to you, and what you want to do.

For a life well-lived, do these things, ordered into some sort of life plan. Raise your children. Give intensity to

REMOVE 90% OF EVERYTHING

your workouts, and vitality to your chosen work and hobbies. Leave a bit of yourself in the things you create. Cultivate deep relationships and love your partner like she's the most important person in the world.

YOUR ENGAGEMENT PATTERNS DETERMINE YOUR DAY

Move towards things that give you energy

You move towards things as a child that light you up and give you energy. I call these engagement patterns. You lose them as an adult, after having been flooded by your parents, teachers, "experts", bosses, media and politicians about how you act, what you should care about, and what you should aim for. Living under engagement patterns forced upon you is a form of tyranny. You are not living in harmony with your being, and so you feel anxiety, dread, stress, purposelessness, and myriad other manifestations. You can re-discover what engages you by auditing your childhood and adolescence, and extracting the qualities present that contributed to you being filled with energy, curiosity and joy, before the grasps of societal programming had gotten a hold of you. These qualities are fundamental to you living a life in alignment with yourself, to be in harmony, to find flow, to find a state of stillness and contentment. You can therefore re-architect your life with effective lifestyle planning, focusing on the few areas that truly matter to you, such as family, health and deep work; and prioritising those energy patterns within them.

Be a detective

When reflecting on your childhood and adolescence, you have to be like a detective to discover the meta-patterns that matter.

For example, when very young, I was restless and always on the move. In later childhood, I found football, and later still, squash and running. Sometimes I'd be in my room, desperately wanting to do things, feeling anxious and frustrated and trapped in restlessness. This is a clear energy pattern. Movement really matters to me. It's fundamental. Whether I'm walking, running, playing squash, or working out; I feel energised when I'm on the move. It expands beyond the physical. If my mind is active on something important to me, I also feel in flow. So, movement is a meta-pattern.

When I was in my room, I mostly liked to be on my own. I'd write, make little poems, draw, daydream, and other similar things. Sometimes as a young adult, I'd go to this gym after work, to the pool. Often, I liked to put my head under water, body floating on the surface, and just be. The noise of the outside world drowned out, I felt a sense of peace and serenity. I liked to go running, somewhere between 3 and 10 miles, and almost always went solo. The same with walks. As a young adult, I'd like to go to coffee shops on my own and read, or journal. The meta-pattern is solitude. I like being on my own for periods of time. Activities like walking, running, working out and writing fulfil that. These periods of 'aloneness', used properly, really energise me. They allow me to do deep work, or allow solutions to

YOUR ENGAGEMENT PATTERNS DETERMINE YOUR DAY

problems to surface, or just let my body, mind and spirit come back into balance. This doesn't mean I don't love my wife, or daughter, or like being with friends, family, community or co-workers. And it doesn't mean I need to live like a monk either. On the contrary, I really enjoy the company of people I love, especially in smaller groups, where we can really connect. But it does mean, to respect my energy patterns, and to live a life in flow and alignment, I should build this meta pattern into parts of my life. I can do this simply and effectively. For example, by doing a daily walk, a workout, and a journaling session during the day. I can also look more deeply into the other parts of my life and see how the energy pattern might compliment those areas. For example, knowing this meta-pattern, I understand that I'm better with less frequent but deeper work communication.

So natural it goes unnoticed

Other meta patterns that come up for me include writing, structure and creativity. Throughout school, I

PART 4 - LESSONS LEARNED

always got great grades in written subjects like English and Religious Studies. I've always journaled, at varying frequencies. As an adult in professional services, I've excelled in writing client reports, figuring out and documenting solutions to problems, clearly and concisely. Writing has always felt easy and natural to me, where other people might struggle. Almost like I'm required to do it at a soul level. A year or so into dating my wife, I remarked to her how my business partner loved fixed routines. She laughed and noted I was the same. I thought of myself as creative and without much structure, yet she detailed how I always run the same couple of routes, always do workout variations of the same basic exercises, mostly eat similar foods, and always need a project to focus on. Upon reflection, that's been the case since adolescence. I realised, it's this structure that allows me to be more creative elsewhere, such as in my work, writing, or travel with family. I like structured games too. Chess has sixty-four squares, a squash court has four walls and a floor. Both

YOUR ENGAGEMENT PATTERNS DETERMINE YOUR DAY

games have constraints, and within both games I like to be both structured and creative.

More energy means you can give more of yourself

I incorporate the engagement patterns that energise me into my weekly life. Because these are all activities I get energy from, I generally feel better, and so can give more of myself in my personal and work relationships. You can do the same, by conducting an audit of your childhood and adolescence, and figuring out the higher order activities or qualities that gave you energy, put you in a state of flow, or brought you joy and contentment. What are the energy patterns you can extract? When did you feel most alive? When did you feel most serene? When were you most engaged? These are signals, unperturbed by the shackles of society and handed down expectations. These are the things you want more of in your life. They are the energy patterns where you are in accord with your being.

Build your energy patterns into your lifestyle design

Once you've figured out these meta patterns, you want to build them into your life as a matter of principle. With lifestyle planning, you choose the categories that matter most to you, and reverse engineer how to get there. As an example, they might be your environment, relationships, deep work, and health and fitness. You might want to live by the sea, get married, start a business, and build muscle. With meta pattern recognition, you're overlaying the best version of your energy alignment so that you're in joy, peace, or content with undertaking your life tasks.

There's overlap between category and meta pattern. For example, health and fitness is a core lifestyle category for me. It arose as a consequence of movement being so fundamental to my being. Deep work is another category. This partially gives me some solitude, structure and creativity, and allows me to express myself with writing and other communication forms. So there's a deep relationship between your lifestyle planning categories, and the meta patterns that give you the most energy, joy and alignment. Done well, your lifestyle categories give you space to express and be in your meta patterns, so that you're living with intention, in a way that lifts you up and feels natural to you.

In paradise, in the desert

With that in mind, you can be in the desert in respect to a part of your life, but in paradise when looking through the lens of your being. Maybe you aren't quite doing the work you want, but if you're managing to be in some of your meta patterns, you can at least derive some joy or interest. Or maybe you're injured in your chosen sport, but knowing your meta patterns, you can still derive energy by shifting to movements you can do.

Your childhood and adolescence hold the secrets to where you get most energy, feel most alive and are in

PART 4 - LESSONS LEARNED

most joy. These are all qualities that will both make you feel more in alignment with your being (and less anxiety and dread), and allow you to be a better person to other people, whether it's your close relationships or wider community. Doing an audit is time well spent. You can quickly improve your day to day life, and create a positive effect on others around you. Out of the desert, into paradise.

LIFESTYLE DESIGN IS ESSENTIAL

Boat without a captain

A boat without a captain will drift at sea, or be swept up in the storms, or crash into the rocks. A plane needs a pilot. A traveller needs a compass. If we don't take the steering wheel of our lives, we'll drift aimlessly into the ether, and wonder where it all went. Or worse, we'll be steered unknowingly, into mundane waters, far from a life we're happy to call our own.

Lifestyle design is plotting what you want your life to look like, and taking steps to get there. It's periodically reviewing where you want to get to, deciding if it's still the right destination, and course correcting if necessary. It's taking control over and responsibility for your life, in order to live it in alignment with your being, so you can make the best of it possible. You only get

PART 4 - LESSONS LEARNED

one go, and it goes by in a flash. So what are you waiting for?

Lifestyle design doesn't remove spontaneity or fun. Instead, it concentrates your most limited resource, time, on the things most important to you; from which purpose, fulfilment, spontaneity and fun can be derived.

Programming, energy, categories

To design an effective life, you begin by removing the programming instilled in you from your childhood, from your peers, and from wider society. Next, audit your childhood, adolescence, and current life for the things that give you energy and fill you up. Figure out the higher order principles at play. I love being in motion, physically and mentally; writing; and periods of solitude. You might like to be still and have lots of group conversations. Now, establish the categories in life most important to you, and how you can integrate the meta patterns that give you energy. For me, it's my

LIFESTYLE DESIGN IS ESSENTIAL

relationships, health and fitness, deep work, and my environment (sun, sea, nature and near a city). For you, it might be surfing in the ocean, cooking, and always being around friends and family.

Take the first step

Now, on your own or with your partner, figure out the steps you can take today, to move towards that lifestyle. If your partner has requirements different from yours, factor those in too. Are there any things you can do that facilitate other parts of your design? My wife and I moved near the sea. I'm a 10 minute drive from my squash club. I can go running or walking by the sea, or in the hills, and find some solitude. I set up a dedicated home office for deep work, and I'm less than an hour's train ride from a major city for key in-person work meetings. My wife walks our daughter by the sea, attends church weekly, has a gym within walking distance, and a home space to record videos for her Youtube channel. These were all intentional choices as part of our lifestyle planning. We made changes to our

PART 4 - LESSONS LEARNED

lives to facilitate this, and we will make more changes in the future as we review, refine and move towards an updated lifestyle design destination. What can you do to get started?

Remove temptations, schedule important things

Once up and running, it's so easy to get distracted. Distracted day-to-day, and distracted from your larger lifestyle design. I'm guilty of this. I think we all are at some point. The amount of times I set up to do deep work, only to find myself scrolling twitter 15 minutes later! With that in mind, it's good to remove things that distract or tempt you, and schedule in the things that matter. For example, if there are donuts in the house, I'm eating them. I have no willpower. I'm the kid raiding the cupboard when no one is watching. And so, we make a point of not buying and keeping that sort of stuff at home. If it's not there, it can't tempt us! And if we do buy it, we don't feel guilty, because we know we're doing the right things most of the time. Or when it comes to deep work, I schedule in a 3-4 hour period from 7am each morning. My wife respects that, and so home distractions are at a minimum, meaning I can get a lot done. In summary, remove the temptations, and schedule in lifestyle design commitments.

Review your plan

Finally, periodically review your lifestyle design, and make amendments. I do this with journaling, and conversations with my wife. Maybe you want to try a new activity. Maybe you're not happy in your environment. Maybe your work is stopping you from doing other things in your life, and you need to find a better solution. Periodic reviews will bring this to light and encourage you to take action on it.

Conclusion

Lifestyle design is essential. What you prioritise as important, and how you go about iterating towards it, will differ from person to person. My best friend loves squash and spending time with his wife. He's decided on a remote-based easy 9-5 developer job that he's the best in the company at, where he gets over 6 weeks holiday and some flexibility in his day schedule. The founders of the start-up I took equity in and sold to UCAS worked round the clock, but had the luxury of choosing what to do after they sold. Each of them had intentions about what they did with their lives and how they spent their time. And ultimately, time is our most scarce resource. It runs out, and you never get it back. Effective lifestyle design will help you to spend it wisely.

TIME IS ALL YOU HAVE

Control over our lives

We all want to be free, to have control over our own lives. And the ultimate freedom is to have control over our time. Time runs out. Everything else is abundant, but we're limited by the number of beats in our heart. We have the most time left from the moment we're born, and it drains away with each passing day. We don't know when the game ends, yet we act like we're going to live forever.

Tyranny is time that's no longer your own. It's doing something you hate, that you didn't purposefully choose to do, over and over again. We all do things we have to do, that we don't want to do, because we have a responsibility to do them. I change my daughter's nappy because she's my responsibility, I'm accountable

PART 4 - LESSONS LEARNED

for her, and I love her. That's different. There's purpose in the task which creates its own sense of fulfilment.

Handing over our time

But most of us accept a life where we hand over our time, whether we know it or not. We give it up to our childhood scripts, to societal programming, and to mimic our peers. We spend hours a day handing over our time, doing things we hate, in exchange for a little money, to buy back some time to make our own. If you're awake, that's why the tyranny of not being in alignment with your being can be so jarring. It's why you feel angst, and stress, and the cortisol flying around your body. It's why you feel tense, when everything closes in around you, and the lights get bright and the sounds are amplified and annoying - it's the moment by moment reminder that your time is not your own, and your time is running out.

Wrong priorities

We chase money, although it's abundant; and yet are flimsy with our time, although it's scarce. We have our priorities backwards. The standard story is to work hard in a job, to save for a retirement, to then do what you love. You give up your precious non-renewable time, for renewable money, in the hope you can buy a little bit of freedom. This is a big risk. You don't know when your clock runs out, and you're gambling you have time left when it finally becomes your own. Do you really want to live a life of drudgery, in the hope you get some joy at the end? What happens if you get sick before you stop? Or you lose money and can't stop? Or you die? What happens then? You don't want to get to the end of your life having never actually taken part in it.

Time paid, and time spent

This is why conscious lifestyle design is so important. It's life or death. You either architect your life to make as much of your time your own, or you willingly give it

PART 4 - LESSONS LEARNED

up and live as a time slave to somebody or something else. You see, not all prisons have walls.

Your life consists of time you have to pay, and time you get to spend. That's it. You fall into the careers you've been programmed to fall into because you think it's a track to attaining money and status. But money is only useful in so much that it buys back your time. Time to love, to play, to explore, to do deep and meaningful projects, to move your body and to relate with your friends and family.

Lifestyle design is adjusting the equation so you get more time as your own. There are many ways to do this. First of all, the design itself means you waste less of your own time on activities that don't fill you up. I prioritise my family, squash, health and fitness, learning and writing, and travel. I do my best not to waste time on things that don't fulfil me, or where I can't be of use.

Lifestyle design and money

When it comes to money, you can work for someone else, do consulting, or build a business. None of these choices are wrong. They depend on your circumstances, and the lifestyle design you're orienting too. Your conscious lifestyle design will inform you. That's what sets you apart.

For you, an easy 9-5 might work, if it means you get to go rock-climbing, or paint, or you can work remotely and travel. You might be willing to accept the time paid and time spent trade-off.

Of course, if you do what you love, work moves from time paid to time spent. Richard Feynman loved physics. There's no way he would have viewed his physics job as time paid. It was likely a joy for him to do the work. Lifestyle design can help you take this track.

Next, there's consulting. If you're super-skilled at something, you can charge more per hour, meaning you need less hours to get more time as your own. If you love the work, even better. But again, even if you don't, the trade-off might be worth it when considering your unique lifestyle design.

I've had success here, in management consulting and executive search. I get to use some of the things I'm drawn to; solving problems in real-time, writing, deep conversations; but I wouldn't choose to do them over writing this book and reaching many people, or playing squash, or being with my wife. I've made myself excellent at the work, so I get to charge a very high rate. I'm paying with time, but I'm earning a high return. This means I get more time to spend on my own. I can architect my weeks, I get to choose where I work from, I get flexibility of lifestyle design. I don't love it, but there are elements I like, and I've found the trade-off worth it to date. Of course, as with a 9-5, if you love the work, if you're in line with your being, then even better - you're not paying with time, you're spending it, and earning money in the process.

TIME IS ALL YOU HAVE

Finally, you can run your own business. Again, if you're doing what you love, and you've planned for it as part of your lifestyle design, then it's time spent, not time paid. If you don't love it, you're effectively betting that you can compress your time paid to earn the right to have the rest of your life to spend time as you see fit. You own the business, you can earn significantly more in profits than you can in a job, and you can sell the business in the future. You can earn enough money in 3-10 years to choose what to do with the rest of the time you have left.

There are many other ways to look at this that the internet has made available. You can run your own business more calmly, trading growth at all costs for effective lifestyle design. You can mix and match the options. I do consulting. I'm writing this book, and others. In the future, I may build a business, if I decide it fits my lifestyle design and value-set, and it's how I want to use my time.

Time is in finite supply

The important thing to remember is that your time is in finite supply. It's never coming back. This moment passed. And this moment. Now this moment. You can't reach back, dust it off, and use it again. It doesn't work like that. Information is abundant. Money is abundant. Time is scarce. Tyranny is having no control over your time. Tyranny is doing things not in alignment with your being, following someone else's program, screaming inside as the seconds of your life tick away. Freedom is re-claiming your time as your own, and spending it on things that light you up and give joy to others. Identifying and removing your scripts helps you to stop doing things that cost you time and don't serve you. Identifying your positive energy patterns show where you get fulfilment spending time. Lifestyle design helps you put that into practice as a process, getting closer and closer to a situation where more of your time is spent doing things that fill you up.

Time is all you have.

DECIDE, TAKE STEPS, ADJUST

Accept where you are today

Reading my story of falling into tyranny and navigating the desert, searching for paradise, might compel you to do the same. Maybe you're on board with removing negative scripts and identifying positive energy patterns. Maybe you know what few things you want to focus your life on. Maybe you've even chatted enthusiastically with your partner about these things with an idea about a life you can move into.

But maybe you're also stuck about how to put this into action. Perhaps you're in a rigid life set-up right now, and it feels impossible to make changes. Maybe you have kids, or a long hours job, or your monthly cash flow is really tight.

PART 4 - LESSONS LEARNED

You have to accept where you are today. Accepting reality for what it is, and taking responsibility for each day thereafter is a huge win for you. I promise. It's moving from tyranny to the desert. It's taking a deep breath, saying, 'okay, here I am, it's time to start moving. I can do this. I will do this, one day at a time, one step at a time.'

Choose what to focus your life on

Now you need to choose what you want to focus your life on, either solo or with a partner. This isn't complicated, and spending weeks on this is a form of procrastination. The things you choose don't have to be for the rest of your life, instead they are the north star you're focusing on now. All plans change on contact with reality, with feedback and understanding. But you need a plan to compare to. So list out the key categories. And pick 1 to 3 activities per category. For example, fitness is a key category of mine. Within it, I choose to do a sport - squash. I choose to do weights workouts (mostly bodyweight, at home). And I choose

DECIDE, TAKE STEPS, ADJUST

to do some running. My relationship with my wife is another. We choose to spend a period of time in the evening together. This takes priority. We choose to be intimate with each other. And we choose to plan trips together over the year, so we can get quality time together, and continue to nurture our relationship.

What are your categories? And what are your priorities within them? Now it might be impossible to reach your destination at once. Accept reality. Then ask yourself the following questions:

- Where are the quick wins?

- Where are the levers?

- What are the biggest bottlenecks?

Quick wins

Quick wins are those things you can do with one or two small changes today. For example, if you want to workout but can't travel to a gym, a quick win is doing sets of pushups and squats 4 times a week. They take

PART 4 - LESSONS LEARNED

10 minutes to do, and you'll start to reap benefits. Or quick wins are things you can do to create space and time to prioritise your lifestyle design. Removal of things are quick wins. Want to be healthier? Get rid of the cakes in the cupboard. Want to spend more time with your wife, or learn Spanish? Remove Netflix and binge watching Youtube videos.

Levers

Levers are the things that when applied, give you big rewards.

A lever for me is my environment. I'm by the sea, near nature, a walk from cafes, a short drive from a squash club, and a short train ride from a city. My environment makes it easy for me to walk, run, have solitude, be in nature, and play sports; all things that are lifestyle design priorities for me. My wife and I moved because when weighing things up, we agreed our current location would better fit our collective lifestyle design. Another lever is my work. I consult, I can work semi-

DECIDE, TAKE STEPS, ADJUST

remotely, I have autonomy, and I have a degree of control over my schedule. This allows me to time block, and gives our family flexibility over travel. So identify the changes you can make that help other pieces of your plan fall into place.

Bottlenecks

Bottlenecks are the obstacles to overcome to move towards a life that's more your own. They are the things that are most holding you back. Common obstacles are debt, work, health and relationships. Some obstacles need tackling head on. If you're sick, you have to prioritise your recovery. This often means removing other things that might be causing you stress. Some obstacles require a multi-pronged attack, or to be circumvented completely. If you're in debt, you need to remove all unnecessary costs, and all unnecessary time sinks. You have to slow your cash outflow, and claw back time, your scarcest resource, so you can make moves to solve the problem. And solving the problem might require bigger thinking. For example, moving to a cheaper location; or re-thinking work, career, or your business. Often, solving for bottlenecks and looking for levers are two sides of the same coin. Maybe you're working for a decent wage but still in debt because your living costs are high. Maybe getting a remote job and moving to a cheaper location helps flip your cash flow from negative to positive. And maybe that location has additional benefits that suit your lifestyle design. And with remote work, maybe you have some extra time to stack skills, or offer consulting, or write a book, or start a business, which will help you develop additional income streams to solve the debt problem faster.

Adjust

And your lifestyle design today doesn't have to be your lifestyle design tomorrow. That's why you review it. You need to periodically check if you've fallen back into your programming, if you're using your positive energy patterns, and if the things you're focusing on are giving you fulfilment. My wife and I have a version of lifestyle

DECIDE, TAKE STEPS, ADJUST

design we're moving into. She's decided on a new category focus activity. I have business and deep work ideas. And we both have a location vision that works for us, creates a great life for our daughter, and keeps us near our core family (another priority). And so, like the method above, we're moving towards it by looking at quick wins, levers and bottlenecks, taking bold steps to turn it into reality.

Decide, take steps, adjust.

CONCLUSION

Practice courage

This personal essay has been an exploration of parts of my life which helped uncover things that were holding me back, or keeping me captured; and a better way I stumbled upon to approach living in alignment with my being.

The subject matter - Who am I? Am I living a life true to myself? What's my purpose? How do I seek fulfilment? - has been discussed for thousands of years.

I'm not inventing anything new - the concept of lifestyle design or lifestyle planning has been discussed extensively in the modern age - and I've borrowed thinking in particular from Tim Ferris and Cal Newport on these things.

CONCLUSION

I hope my personal experiences, what I learned, and how I cobbled together different ideas to approach life, are of service to you. I hope you see that tyranny starts in the prison of the mind, with bars made of childhood programming, peer pressure and societal expectations. And that moving from tyranny to the desert is hard. It's one of the hardest things you can do, because it means moving from certainty to the unknown, and the unknown is scary. But it also means taking responsibility for your life, practising courage, steering your ship, and owning the consequences. If you have an idea of where you want to go, and you plot a route to it, this can be deeply fulfilling.

Recap

I started by discussing my childhood scripts. How I had a complicated relationship with my dad, and how I was desperate to please him. My life choices were in service of that goal, and I didn't know it. And I lacked courage and know-how to do anything different. I pursued a career in accountancy, living every day with my

PART 4 - LESSONS LEARNED

stomach in knots. I thought I had to be a somebody. I thought I had to make Partner, and have status, and build wealth in a mundane, boring way. I thought this was life and it's just how it was and that I was ungrateful for feeling differently.

I then wrote about how I couldn't shake the feeling of angst. That this wasn't the life for me, that this couldn't be all there was. How I could sense my mental tyranny, and how I quit my career when my Dad moved overseas. I had no idea what I was doing, and unbeknown to me, I'd fallen into the desert. I had a failed recruitment business, I dabbled in e-commerce, and I reverted to business consulting, which culminated in a large turnaround project. During this time, I fell deep into the void. I remember one day staring at my tiny living room walls, and just screaming, because I had no idea of who I was and what I was supposed to be doing, and I felt like I was wasting my life. I didn't know what to do, and I didn't know where to turn for guidance. However, without realising, I was building

CONCLUSION

lots of skills, and a deep resilience. Business consulting took me out of the void. It gave me a platform where I could perform. It wasn't a life in alignment, but it was momentum. And I was good at it. I then went travelling and became a digital nomad. I was still in the desert, and I was trying on the hats of different authors and online personalities. The detachment from normal space and the free time created a solitude where I could reflect. I had peace. I started to see the childhood scripts at play. I couldn't verbalise it. But I could feel it. I could better sense what to move towards and what to move away from, although I was far away from having a compass or any solid intention.

Then I quickly lost my dad. Diagnosis to death in six weeks. And it was jarring. I went into denial with a false stoicism. But in truth, it plunged me into a void. I kept applying for and turning down jobs. Great jobs too, but something was stopping me. I lost hours to coffee shops, dwindling away savings, reading blogs and brainstorming business ideas and generally screaming

PART 4 - LESSONS LEARNED

inside with anxiety and dread. I was in the same mental space as before, back in the tiny living room, but magnified. Losing my Dad cut my tether to my existing path. It threw me into disarray. It made me question everything. Who I was, what I wanted, and what choices were for me.

Seeing a therapist was a slow catalyst for change. But there was a difficult decision that took another 18 months to make. In the meantime, I got myself into executive search and business consulting. I had motion, and motion creates momentum. It's during this time I started paying attention to my positive energy patterns, and my talents, and extrapolating where the more intentional application of both could take me. I was accumulating skills and experiences, making connections, building courage, and moving forwards. Journalling accelerated this. It helped me to uncover limiting patterns of behaviour, reflect on my life more deeply, and take my first steps into intentional lifestyle design.

CONCLUSION

I had a step-change in momentum and took some more key life decisions. I was prioritising work, health and fitness. I took on additional consulting work, learned and applied more skills, and helped more people. Covid lockdown gave me a forced solitude. In this time, I took small equity in and helped sell a nearly pre-revenue start-up. When not doing that, I was working out or walking. When not doing that, I was journalling and uncovering insights about myself and about my life.

Next, I fell in love. I found my soulmate. And through love and relationship, I got a new perspective to my life. Through conversation and reflection, I got serious about lifestyle design, what matters to me (and now us), and how to go about designing for it. Love pulls you out of tyranny. It can uncover your negative scripts, highlight your positive energy patterns, and unearth a north star for you to aim for.

Then I became a Dad myself, and see it as the greatest privilege in the world. We had a harrowing start. Nearly

PART 4 - LESSONS LEARNED

losing your soul mate and child sharply puts life into perspective, and makes a mockery of all the things you thought were important. And children become a forcing function. The chaos raising a child can bring, forces you to either get carried by the tide, or get really focused on deciding what you want your life to look like, and taking action to make it happen.

Having a child gave me new perspectives. My wife had carried and incubated my daughter for 9 months. We care and nurture her every day. It's given us a long-term time horizon. And it's our relationship to her that makes it so meaningful. I realised, by putting a piece of my soul into things, life becomes rich, vivid, and very fulfilling. This extends beyond the literal - children - and into all areas of life. It's the way you interact in your relationships. It's how you play a sport. It's this book. It's taking you from angst and self-obsession to doing something that impacts others through self-expression.

This is amplified with faith in a higher power. My wife taught me faith. Faith is letting something greater than

CONCLUSION

you into your heart to guide you, giving you courage to take action, with perspective, over the long term, in accordance with a higher standard. It's a guiding force. It's fuel that takes you out of your mental tyranny and into the desert; out of the stands and onto the court. It gives you a longer-term perspective, a code to follow in times of uncertainty, courage to take decisions, and momentum as you move into the unknown. It's a pull to life, to vitality.

And in this life, what's essential is invisible to the eye. Our relationships and responsibilities to people, to things, and to ourselves, are the foundations of everything. With strength in these things, you can have a breakthrough life. Without strength; tyranny. Relationship and responsibility gives us meaning and makes things unique to us because, in effect, we are embedding ourselves into them. To relate well to anything – whether it's your partner, your work, your health – takes time.

And time is the most scarce asset we have. We have the most we'll ever have at birth, and a decreasing amount each day. We don't know when it runs out, and we don't get much advance warning when it does. And as far as we know, we only get one go on this earth. Therefore, planning and living a life in accordance with your being, maximising your energy flows, doing things that fulfil you, and positively impacting those around you, seems to be the best thing you can do. It's living with intention. It's moving out of tyranny, into the desert, heading towards paradise.

Breakthrough life

Without intention and action, you succumb to programming, conformity and stasis. You are not living your own life. You must identify these things, remove them, and replace them with conscious lifestyle design in order to live a breakthrough life.

You live a breakthrough life by identifying the energy patterns that most uplift you, the categories most

CONCLUSION

important to you, and the priorities within them. You design for what's essential, and take steps to reach it. You go deep on things, building relationships with them, taking responsibility for them, and giving a piece of yourself to them. You love, which is life force itself. And you have faith. Faith in a higher power guiding you. Faith as you navigate the desert. Faith and the courage of your convictions that you are on the right path and you can indeed live a breakthrough life.

Thank you for reading.

ABOUT THE AUTHOR

Joe Thomsett is a writer, husband, father, fitness enthusiast and entrepreneur.

You can learn more about him at https://joethomsett.com

He helps his wife grow her YouTube channel, encouraging people to workout and get fit - https://www.youtube.com/@AniaThomsett

Finally, go to https://breakthrough.community for Breakthrough books, to attend Breakthrough retreats, and to join the Breakthrough digital community.

Other Links:

Instagram: https://www.instagram.com/itsjoethomsett/
Linkedin: https://www.linkedin.com/in/joethomsett/

> If there's something in the book that impacted you, I'd love it if you could leave an honest Amazon review for others to see.
>
> Thank you.
>
> Love, Joe.

NOTES

https://breakthrough.community

NOTES

https://breakthrough.community

NOTES

https://breakthrough.community

NOTES

https://breakthrough.community

Printed in Great Britain
by Amazon